The Rhetoric Companion

THE RHETORIC COMPANION

A Student's Guide to Power in Persuasion

N. D. WILSON

DOUGLAS WILSON

canonpress
Moscow, Idaho

Published by Canon Press
P. O. Box 8729, Moscow, ID 83843
800–488–2034 | www.canonpress.com

N. D. Wilson and Douglas Wilson, *The Rhetoric Companion:*
A Student's Guide to Power in Persuasion
Copyright © 2011 by N. D. Wilson and Douglas Wilson.

Unless noted otherwise, all Scripture references are taken from the Authorized Version.

Cover design by Rachel Rosales.
Interior design by Laura Storm.

Printed in the United States of America.

Library of Congress Cataloging-in-Publication Data

Wilson, Douglas, 1953-
    The rhetoric companion : a student's guide to power in persuasion / N.D. Wilson,
Douglas Wilson.
       p. cm.
    ISBN-13: 978-1-59128-078-1 (pbk.)
    ISBN-10: 1-59128-078-8 (pbk.)
 1. English language--Rhetoric. 2. Report writing. 3. Academic writing. I. Wilson, Nathan D. II. Title.
    PE1408.W6148 2011
    808'.042--dc22

                          2010028649

 12 13 14 15 16 17 18 19 20   10 9 8 7 6 5 4 3 2

Contents

Introduction

The first question to ask and answer would be, "What exactly is *The Rhetoric Companion*?" And a related question might be, "Why do I need it?"

This text is designed for students of classical rhetoric who are old enough to drive, and young enough to still be breathing. As a stand-alone text, it can be used over the course of a term or semester. As a supplement or "companion," it can be used in conjunction with some of the historic texts for the study of classic rhetoric, extended over the course of a year. At the conclusion of every chapter, the student will find suggested readings from texts like the *Rhetorica Ad Herennium* or Quintilian's *Institutio Oratoria*. The best (or at least the fullest) use of this text will be as a companion to accompany the modern student in his readings of these ancient texts. If a student does all the readings, when the course is done, he will have read through Aristotle's *Rhetoric*, the *Rhetorica Ad Herennium*, and all of Quintilian. Because of the nature of the case, these readings will not always correspond to the lessons, but there should usually be some level of interrelated relevance. The references will all be to the Loeb editions of these books, cited by book, chapter, and section.

At the same time, this text also seeks to incorporate two other sources of information about rhetoric—one foundational and the other more current and contemporary. The foundational issues are biblical—Christian writers were wrestling with how classical rhetoric intersected with Christian faith as early as Augustine's *On Christian Doctrine*. The answers that Christians have offered have varied, but over the centuries a

How can we conceive of any real eloquence at all proceeding from a man who is ignorant of all that is best in the world? —**Quintilian,** *Institutio Oratoria, vol. 4*[1]

I. All quotations from Quintilian are taken from *Institutio Oratoria*, 4 vols., trans. H. E. Butler (Cambridge: Harvard University Press, 1920–1922).

Without natural gifts, technical rules are useless. Consequently, the student who is devoid of talent will derive no more profit from this work than barren soil from a treatise on agriculture.
—**Quintilian,** *Institutio Oratoria, vol. 1*

consensus has emerged, thanks largely to Augustine. One ancient writer compared a Christian use of classical learning to an Israelite who saw a beautiful foreigner taken captive in war. He was allowed to marry her, but only after she had grieved the loss of her family and had been purged of all her pagan cultural trappings (Deut. 21:11). Her beauty was real, but so was the danger. Another common comparison was to the way the children of Israel left Egypt with a great deal of Egypt's wealth. Since that time, many believers have defended their appropriation and use of unbelieving culture with that particular phrase—"plundering the Egyptians." Unfortunately, this phrase is frequently used by Christians to defend the inputting of massive amounts of grimy media into one's skull. (That's more like dumpster diving in Egypt than plundering. The Israelites did not each give eight dollars to the girl in the ticket booth so that they could go in and look at the Egyptians' gold.) The ancient Christian writers had more of a grasp of what plundering was actually supposed to look like. Now as more and more classical Christian schools are flourishing, the question of what to do with "the gold" has arisen again. This text will seek to bring every aspect of the ancient discipline of rhetoric to the bar of Scripture.

The second issue has to do with how much the world has changed since the time of Cicero. What does rhetoric mean in a world of Facebook and Twitter, and how can an eloquent argument survive in an era of sound bytes and bumper stickers and one-handed thumb typing? In some ways the question points to a real dilemma—a great deal of our public discourse these days really is coarse and cheap, and politicians really are trained to not answer questions. But at the same time, the modern era is sometimes dismissed too readily. A bumper sticker or a tweet certainly can represent mere sloganeering, and the paucity of words often corresponds to the poverty of thought. However, short, pithy phrases have gone into the commonplace books of rhetoricians for centuries, and there is no reason why we should reject them out of hand. That being said, modern students have to make some mental adjustments as they seek to translate the classic principles of ancient rhetoric to the digital age. Would Cicero have had a blog? And if so, would it have been any good?

So this text is offered in the conviction that God in His common grace bestowed a great deal of practical wisdom about public discourse on the ancient practitioners of rhetoric. However, this cannot simply be assumed—we have to hold what they taught up against the final standard of Scripture. At the same time, we have to compare what they taught about a speech in a city forum, without microphones, to this age of global YouTubery. Unless we distinguish principles and methods, we will find ourselves using quill pens instead of laptops, and all because we are hung up on the particular methods of the dead.

With that said, at least, let us begin.

> The road may be pointed out, but our speed must be our own.
> —**Quintilian,** *Institutio Oratoria, vol. 3*

SUGGESTED READING

    1. Aristotle, *The Rhetoric and the Poetics of Aristotle* (New York: McGraw-Hill, 1984), I.1.1-11.8

Biblical Wisdom and Rhetoric

The study and practice of rhetoric is regarded today with an almost universal suspicion, from Christians and non-Christians alike. And why wouldn't we all be suspicious? In the modern world the word *rhetoric* smells like campaign lies, late night infomercials (only seventeen easy payments . . .), and every other type of self-interested manipulation. But for Christians the standard must always be, from beginning to end, the Word of God. If Scripture condemns thought-out and practiced rhetoric, then so should we. If it does not, then we have no basis for any real or abiding complaint. There are many subjects of study (like history or mathematics) that do not have to begin with a justification of their pursuit. But there are others where suspicion runs deep (rhetoric, philosophy, palm-reading, etc.).

Where does this almost universal suspicion of rhetoric come from? Is this a biblical suspicion, a suspicion of a legitimate pursuit now long-abused, a pagan suspicion of cultural maturity? If the latter, have Christians simply picked up this suspicion from the world? Or perhaps it is some tangled combination of all of the above? Suspicion of rhetoric goes back at least to the time of Socrates, but note what this does. Socrates was a pagan, just like the sophists were. Perhaps our *suspicion* of rhetoric is something we got from paganism also.

Rhetoric as a formal subject is the third part of the classical Trivium—grammar, dialectic and then *rhetoric*. It is almost at the halfway point in the seven liberal arts, the last four being the Quadrivium—arithmetic, geometry, astronomy, and music. As a *formal* subject of study, it attracts less opposition. But as an *informal* whipping boy, rhetoric has become synonymous with "sophistry," meaning some kind of chicanery with words, or empty rhetoric. "That's a bunch of rhetoric" would never

At any rate let us banish from our hearts the delusion that eloquence, the fairest of all things, can be combined with vice.
—**Quintilian,** *Institutio Oratoria, vol. 4*

I hold that no one can be a true orator unless he is also a good man, and, even if he could be, I would not have it so.
—**Quintilian,** *Institutio Oratoria, vol. 1*

be mistaken for a positive statement. As just mentioned, this suspicion goes back at least to Socrates, who had a great deal of trouble with the sophists (mercenary tongues and brains for hire). We should share his suspicion of the emptiness there, but we should also remember that the suspicion was just as pagan in its origins as was the object of suspicion. Both sides were already in play in the ancient world.

With this popular understanding of "empty rhetoric" providing us with a starting place, consider some of the things the Bible says which actually do condemn it. St. Paul addresses rhetorical issues explicitly. The passage is the *locus classicus* on this subject, and so it is worth quoting at length. Some of the key phrases and relevant portions have been italicized.

> For Christ sent me not to baptize, but to preach the gospel: *not with wisdom of words,* lest the cross of Christ should be made of none effect. For the preaching of the cross is to them that perish foolishness; but unto us which are saved it is the power of God. For it is written, I will destroy the wisdom of the wise, and will bring to nothing the understanding of the prudent. Where is the wise? where is the scribe? *where is the disputer of this world?* hath not God made foolish the wisdom of this world? For after that in the wisdom of God the world by wisdom knew not God, it pleased God by the foolishness of preaching to save them that believe. For the Jews require a sign, and the Greeks seek after wisdom: But we preach Christ crucified, unto the Jews a stumblingblock, and unto the Greeks foolishness; But unto them which are called, both Jews and Greeks, Christ the power of God, and the wisdom of God. Because the foolishness of God is wiser than men; and the weakness of God is stronger than men. For ye see your calling, brethren, how that not many wise men after the flesh, not many mighty, not many noble, are called: But God hath chosen the foolish things of the world to confound the wise; and God hath chosen the weak things of the world to confound the things which are mighty; And base things of the world, and things which are despised, hath God chosen, yea, and things which are not, to bring to nought things that are: That no flesh should glory in his presence. But of him are ye in Christ Jesus, who of God is made unto us wisdom, and righteousness, and sanctification, and redemption: That, according as it is written, He that glorieth, let him glory in the Lord. And I, brethren, when I came to you, *came not with excellency of speech or of*

wisdom, declaring unto you the testimony of God. For I determined not to know any thing among you, save Jesus Christ, and him crucified. And I was with you in weakness, and in fear, and in much trembling. And my speech and my preaching was *not with enticing words of man's wisdom,* but in demonstration of the Spirit and of power: That your faith should not stand in the wisdom of men, but in the power of God. Howbeit *we speak wisdom* among them that are perfect: *yet not the wisdom of this world,* nor of the princes of this world, that come to nought: But we speak the wisdom of God in a mystery, even the hidden wisdom, which God ordained before the world unto our glory: Which none of the princes of this world knew: for had they known it, they would not have crucified the Lord of glory. But as it is written, "Eye hath not seen, nor ear heard, neither have entered into the heart of man, the things which God hath prepared for them that love him." But God hath revealed them unto us by his Spirit: for the Spirit searcheth all things, yea, the deep things of God. For what man knoweth the things of a man, save the spirit of man which is in him? even so the things of God knoweth no man, but the Spirit of God. Now we have received, not the spirit of the world, but the spirit which is of God; that we might know the things that are freely given to us of God. *Which things also we speak, not in the words which man's wisdom teacheth,* but which the Holy Ghost teacheth; comparing spiritual things with spiritual. (I Cor. 1:17–2:13)

Christians must obviously condemn what Paul here condemns and praise what he praises. Paul rejects the "wisdom of words," the "disputing of this world," "excellency in speech or wisdom," or "enticing words of man's wisdom." He contrasts all this with preaching Christ and the "foolishness" of preaching.

In a word, Paul is rejecting human *autonomy* in rhetoric. He is opposing every form of humanism in the art of using words well. But when we have rejected that autonomy, the myth of neutrality, does this mean that Christians must actively seek to stumble over their words? Is Paul himself clumsy with his words, or does he communicate effectively and powerfully? Does godliness mean we must cultivate a lisp or a distracting stammer? Should every preacher of the gospel, if he is to be faithful to

Eloquent speakers give pleasure, wise ones salvation.
—**Saint Augustine,** *On Christian Teaching*[1]

I. All quotations from Saint Augustine are taken from *On Christian Teaching* (Oxford: Oxford University Press, 1999).

Given a sharp and eager mind, eloquence is picked up more readily by those who read and listen to the words of the eloquent than by those who follow the rules of eloquence.
—**Saint Augustine,** *On Christian Teaching*

We easily escape the seeming disclaimer of the great Apostle, by asking what was that rhetoric which he repudiated, and whether he did not employ a method of his own? The Christian antiquary answers the first question. The spurious and unworthy art which is here rejected, was that of the Greek Sophists—a system of mere tricks of logic and diction, prompted by vanity and falsehood, and misguided by a depraved taste.
—**R. L. Dabney,** *Sacred Rhetoric*[2]

this passage, seek to bumble around in the pulpit on purpose? (Some do, oddly.) No, of course not. But preachers and teachers and every Christian called to communicate (which is every Christian) still have to do *something* with this passage.

The foolishness of preaching. The foolishness of the cross, of humility, of stooping. Forget the "enticing words of man's wisdom." Christ (and His apostles) retooled effective communication and rhetoric. Let another praise you and not your own lips. No more ancient, self-praising, pagan rhetors chest-thumping like rappers. And perhaps most importantly, no longer is "convincing" one's opponents the measure of success or failure. Christ functioned differently—"foolishly"—and so should we.

Definitions of rhetoric vary in the classical writers, but adapting one of them, with a peculiarly Christian backdrop and understanding, provides us with our working definition of rhetoric: *the art of a good man speaking well.* This definition has two clear evaluative terms in it, *good* and *well.* Whenever we hear words like this, we should realize that a particular standard is being assumed and applied, and we should always be asking what standard that is. What is a *good* man? And what does it mean to speak *well?* Such evaluative terms have to be defined in accordance with the teaching of Scripture.

The follower of Christ should learn how to speak honestly and plainly, with those terms understood scripturally. For the justification of this claim, it is only necessary to consider again the passage quoted earlier. But the Christian must also speak appealingly. "The thoughts of the wicked are an abomination to the LORD: but the words of the pure are pleasant words" (Prov. 15:26). It is important to speak thoughtfully and deliberately. "Seest thou a man that is hasty in his words? there is more hope of a fool than of him" (Prov. 29:20). And of course, one must speak appropriately—"A word fitly spoken is like apples of gold in pictures of silver" (Prov. 25:11).

For the believer, manipulative sophistry is clearly out of bounds. But putting careful thought into what constitutes pleasant and appropriate words is not. What many people dismiss as "a bunch of rhetoric" is simply *poor* rhetoric. In the classical world, there were not a few "speech

2. *Sacred Rhetoric* (Carlisle: Banner of Truth, 1979), 17.

instructors" who were willing to teach their students to lie, cheat, and cry, if it would only help them get their way or to win their case in court—a lot like today, in fact. Such dishonesty is completely inconsistent with a Christian approach to rhetoric and communication. But nevertheless, there is a Christian approach to rhetoric, and to a development of that approach we now turn. To the extent that the classical rhetoricians opposed empty sophistry, we join them in blowing dismissive raspberries. To the extent that they accommodated themselves to that same sophistry, we must kick them to the side and move on to cultivate a distinctively biblical approach to *the art of a good man speaking well.*

SUGGESTED READING

1. Aristotle, *Rhetoric,* I.II.9—III.6.
2. Quintilian, *Institutio Oratoria,* vol. I, trans. H. E. Butler (Cambridge: Harvard University Press, 1920), I.Greeting—IV.16.

EXERCISE

1. Find twenty-five short, well-written excerpts from any outside reading and copy them (with citation) into a commonplace book. Select the strongest ten and work on delivering them orally until you can do them justice. Introduce and deliver them publicly.

REVIEW QUESTIONS

1. Where does the almost universal suspicion of rhetoric come from?
2. Is this a biblical suspicion?
3. What is the position of rhetoric in the Trivium?
4. What is the Quadrivium?
5. What is sophistry?
6. Does I Corinthians 1:17–2:13 require Christians to reject rhetoric? Why or why not?

The Purposes of Rhetoric

What is rhetoric *for?* In a world where everyone was knowledgeable, agreed about everything, and was always prepared to do the right thing, rhetoric would be unnecessary. (Maybe.) But alas, that is not the case, and so here we are, studying rhetoric. The point of true rhetoric, in all its guises, is to deal with ignorance, bring about like-mindedness, and motivate to action. In stating this, we must not allow biblical standards to slip away from us. We must deal with ignorance as the Bible would define it; we should strive to bring about like-mindedness in the truth; and we should be motivating the listeners to right action.

[handwritten margin note: point of rhetoric]

But this is still too general. The specific purposes of rhetoric will vary with the occasion. Depending on where you are, you will speak in different ways in order to get a good result.

Aristotle taught that rhetoric was the "power of discovering the possible means of persuasion in reference to any subject whatever."[1] Although Aristotle might complain we are engaged in gnat-strangling, his definition is not quite adequate. Someone could be an effective rhetor under this definition without ever saying anything. A cute girl winking can be very persuasive, but we wouldn't normally call that rhetoric. A man could discover the possible means of persuasion without using any typical oratorical means. Also, we have the problem of certain activities that can be *very* persuasive that we wouldn't want to classify as rhetoric—for example, sending Guido around to break someone's kneecaps, sexual blackmail or seduction, bribery, and so forth.

Then there is the problem of limiting rhetoric to the *discovery* of the means of persuasion. A man could sit around in his sweatpants

> The task of the public speaker is to discuss capably those matters which law and custom have fixed for the uses of citizenship, and to secure as far as possible the agreement of his hearers.
> —**Harry Caplan,** introduction to the *Rhetorica Ad Herennium*[2]

1. *Rhetoric,* I.2
2. All quotations from the *Rhetorica Ad Herennium* are taken from the Harvard University Press edition (Cambridge, 1954).

My aim, then, is the education of the perfect orator. The first essential for such an one is that he should be a good man, and consequently we demand of him not merely the possession of exceptional gifts of speech, but of all the excellences of character as well.
—**Quintilian,** *Institutio Oratoria, vol. 1*

doing that and never speak to anyone (or even blog). This definition of rhetoric appears to be a good definition for the first of the five canons of rhetoric—invention. It is through the process of invention that we discover the "available means of persuasion."

The definition in the previous chapter is Quintilian's. The rhetorician is a good person, speaking well. This excludes the glib demagogue—at least if we remember our ethical basis for the term "good." Further, this definition requires that we actually speak. But speaking well *how?* Where? Upon what sorts of occasions?

There are three kinds of rhetoric in the older classification, so let us begin with the ancient categories. These are judicial, deliberative, and epideictic.

JUDICIAL—The point in this form of rhetoric is to determine guilt or innocence. This is a significant part of Roman rhetoric, with their characteristic emphasis on courts of law. You would think that courtroom oratory would be important in our culture, but it is not, largely because of the procedures we have developed that enable us to establish (or circumvent, as the case may be) justice. Courtrooms are very important in our society, but now they are largely bureaucratically driven and manipulated by preemptive filings and motions. Oratory in our time rarely rises above "if it doesn't fit, you must acquit."

DELIBERATIVE—Should we go left or right? "Deliberative speeches are either of the kind in which the question concerns a choice between two courses of action, or of the kind in which a choice among several is considered."[3] This is the kind of oratory that is employed when an important bill is being debated in the legislature, or when a church congregation is trying to decide whether to hold a potluck this Tuesday or the next.

EPIDEICTIC—Is the guy under discussion a hero or a toad? Epideictic speeches are concerned with praise or blame. Here we can clearly see the relevance of our "by what standard" standard. The standards of the

3. *Rhetorica Ad Herennium,* III.II.2.

classical world dictated what was considered worthy of praise or blame. "The following, then, can be subject to praise: External Circumstances, Physical Attributes, and Qualities of Character."[4] In the world today (thanks to the "foolishness" to which Paul was referring), serious praise would be reserved for the last category only. Praise in the first two categories, in our day, would be limited to puff pieces in *People* magazine. People still do it, but it is considered gossip in print and not a serious use of words.

So these are the ancient categories. But there have been Christian developments since then. The handling of the word of God in preaching has brought in a separate category. The ancient world had those individuals who spoke for the gods, but they had to be possessed or stoned or both in order for this to happen. A Christian minister speaks the word of the living God, and this changes everything. "[I]t applies to the will, the authority of God, the only Lord of the conscience."[5] In other words, Christian preaching and teaching claims to be able to bind the conscience authoritatively; the claim being made is an explicit authority to command in the name of God. So not only do we have the additional category created by "the sermon," we also have additional types of public talks that owe something of their structure to the delivery of sermons over the centuries—modern political speeches would be one example. In a very real way, this binding of the conscience introduces a distinctly Christian understanding of proof—to prove something is not to establish infallible mathematical certainty; it is to obligate belief.

Remember that categories like this (that is, preaching and teaching) cannot be considered watertight. But these are two additional categories where rhetorical wisdom is called for. The first is preaching—the word of God is proclaimed by men, both to nonbelievers and to the saints. This is proclamation of what is called the *kerygma*, that which is set before us in order to be believed by us, the *credenda*. Then there is teaching, in which the word of God is expounded by men—the statement of the *didache*. That which is to be done is the *agenda*.

4. *Rhetorica Ad Herennium*, III.VI.10.
5. Dabney, *Sacred Rhetoric*, 34.

The classic writer does not have to persuade the reader. All he has to do is offer the reader an unobstructed view, and of course the reader will see.

—**Francis-Noel Thomas and Mark Turner,** *Clear and Simple as the Truth*[6]

It may be noticed that missing from the list of preaching and teaching is the notion of a dry recital of data, the better to help you get your degree with. *The Matrix* notwithstanding, we cannot download data into our heads and expect to come away with true understanding. This "computer printout" approach to facts does happen in too many classrooms but cannot be considered in the study of rhetoric, except as a failure or an example to be avoided.

Purpose of rhetoric

The purpose of rhetoric is to persuade men to believe and act in a manner consistent with whatever the circumstances require. If they are jurors, should they vote to acquit or not? If legislators, should they vote yes or no? If they are congregants, how should their lives be different over the course of the next week?

Let us expand our definition somewhat. A rhetor is a good man speaking well. But in a Christian context, what does it mean to be a *good* man? And does that context change anything about what it means to speak well? We should therefore say that a rhetor must be a *godly* man, speaking well in his attempt to persuade others to believe and act in accordance with biblical wisdom.

This a distinctively Christian definition because we live in a distinctively Christian world.

SUGGESTED READING

1. Aristotle, *Rhetoric*, I.III.7—V.7.
2. Quintilian, *Institutio Oratoria*, vol. I, I.IV.17—VII.27.

EXERCISE

1. Collect twenty-five more short excerpts for your commonplace book. Choose the most striking of the batch and make it your own in a composition. While trying to match the tone and voice of the quote, add 150–200 of your own words.

6. All quotations by Francis-Noel Thomas and Mark Turner are taken from *Clear and Simple as the Truth* (Princeton: Princeton University Press, 1994), 51.

REVIEW QUESTIONS

1. What is the definition of rhetoric we are using in this book? How does the Christian faith affect the definition?
2. What are the three purposes of rhetoric?
3. What was Aristotle's definition of rhetoric? Are there any problems with it?
4. What are the three kinds of rhetoric in the ancient classification?
5. Have there been any developments "in kinds" since then?

Basic Copiousness

Copiousness comes at the very beginning of the study of rhetoric, and it is the capstone at the end. It provides foundational material, and it enables the speaker overflow in a way that is rhetorically compelling. In a very real sense, copiousness refers to the stuff or material of speaking—what one has to say. Handled rightly, it also improves how one says it.

But let us make an important distinction. In this small book, we are using the term *commonplaces* in two different ways, although they are somewhat related. The first use comes from the Latin (*locis communis*), and refers to the commonly-held worldview phrases circulated in every community. "Think globally, act locally" is an environmentalist commonplace in this sense. A Christian commonplace would be something like, "hate the sin, love the sinner." But remember, something can be a commonplace, even a Christian commonplace, and not be right. A commonplace is a proverb or a striking phrase at the acceptable end and a cliché at the unacceptable end. If it is false, then it becomes a lying cliché.

The second sense of commonplace is how we are using it in the phrase *commonplace book.* In your commonplace book, you should be collecting quotations, phrases, and poems to aid the flow of your own copiousness and to influence your own voice. Some of the items in your collection will probably also be commonplaces in the first sense. Collect them in order to use them.

First, the principle. The Bible teaches us, with regard to finances, that the one who sows sparingly will also reap sparingly. This is a commonplace that applies to commonplaces. Applying this to public speaking, we can readily see that if someone has not taken very much in, there will not be very much that can come out. A hollow jug cannot pour for very

For a long time . . . we should read none save the best authors and such as are least likely to betray our trust in them.
—**Quintilian,** *Institutio Oratoria, vol. 4*

long. When we talk here about achieving copiousness, we are talking about how best to fill the jug.

But before considering how to fill the jug, a few corks for the top of the jug have to be thrown away. So before we talk about what to do, we'll consider a few words about what *not* to do. Many Christian writers take a dim view of much of modern entertainment—movies, sitcoms, foul lyrics in pop songs, and so on—for moral reasons. Without taking anything away from their concern, which is legitimate, there is also a linguistic reason to avoid modern entertainment: too much eye candy will wreck one's ability to speak in coherent sentences. And if rhetoric is being studied, such an inability is a bad thing. Related to this, the slack lifestyle that accompanies the kind of fellow who rents ten videos for one weekend is not conducive to acquiring anything worthwhile to say. If you listen to stupid music, watch stupid movies, and read stupid books . . . well, congratulations, you're stupid. And, being stupid, you have failed in the pursuit of effective communication at the outset.

Achieving copiousness is the result of an ongoing discipline with words, which is nevertheless thoroughly enjoyable. Some suggestions follow for those who would be copious in an educated way.

Read the Bible—of course, Christians should read the Bible in a good translation. But entirely apart from the textual and spiritual arguments, if someone is not thoroughly acquainted with the Authorized Version (and this means repeatedly reading the whole thing), then that individual is not educated. He might be clever and trained, but not educated in the historical categories of our culture. The Authorized Version (popularly known as the King James) is one of the great literary achievements of our culture. If you want to build a great mansion or cathedral, it will be necessary to take a goodly bit of rock from *this* quarry.

Read good books—if a man becomes a vidiot, then he will accumulate dross in his conversation. He will be able to quote Jim Carrey or Adam Sandler or Batman, but that is the end of his library. But if a man mines where many others have found gold and silver, he will soon find that these are mines that do not get depleted. The more they are read, the more they yield. A small sampling of the kind of writers who have given inspiration to many would include G. K. Chesterton, C. S. Lewis, H. L. Mencken, Tom Wolfe, P. G. Wodehouse, and others.

For without the consciousness of such preliminary study, our powers of speaking extempore will give us nothing but an empty flow of words, springing from the lips and not from the brain.
—**Quintilian,** *Institutio Oratoria, vol. 4*

Read a lot of books—over the course of years our rhetoric students at New St. Andrews College got into the habit of reading one to two (good) books a week. When someone acquires and maintains such a habit over time, it amounts to copiousness. Twenty years of a book a week probably adds up to having something available to say. And having worthy material at the ready is what copiousness is.

Read dictionaries (no joke)—collect words. Collecting memorable phrases is a profitable activity, but the world is also full of words which describe what you see in new and interesting ways. Read dictionaries, a page a day, and there are many to choose from. Read dictionaries of slang, of defunct Welsh playground insults from the eighteenth century, of proverbs, of foreign words and phrases, of little-known words, and even regular old dictionaries. Dictionary readers would probably have known what a chad was before the election tangle in 2000. But at the same time, eschew prolixity.

Read aloud to yourself—and in this reading, make a point of listening to the cadences of words. This is the point of reading poetry aloud, but the same principle can be observed in good prose writers. You want to develop an ear for prose that clanks. Also, reading aloud can reveal a problem in your own composition that was inoffensive on paper when you first wrote it down but will surely trip you up when you try to say it.

Mark or record any hot stuff—put it down in your commonplace book, or mark it in the book in such a way that you will be able to find it again readily.

Make a point of using what you learn—if you put a quote from Winston Churchill down in your commonplace book, don't just leave it there. Look for an opportunity to *use* it—in a paper, in a speech, in a conversation. If you write it down and use it several times, then you will very likely remember it.

The effects of copiousness can be significant. One important principle in speaking is to always leave an audience wanting to hear more from you, not less. Part of this means clearly having more that you *could* say if necessary. If you stop when you could go on, this will be evident to the listener. If you continue ten minutes past the point when you ran out of things to say, this will be equally (and painfully) obvious. Finish

The sum of the whole matter is this: write quickly and you will never write well, write well and you will soon write quickly.
—**Quintilian,** *Institutio Oratoria, vol. 4*

early, not late. Stop unloading the truck while there is still stuff on it. Don't continue unloading when the truck has been empty for the last ten minutes.

Play with words. Juggle them. Write them down. Roll in them. Bake them into cookies. Quote them. Remember them. And such richness in the vocabulary of discourse does accumulate.

In every discipline artistic theory is of little avail without unremitting exercise.
—*Rhetorica Ad Herennium*

SUGGESTED READING

1. Aristotle, *Rhetoric*, I.V.8—VI.30
2. Quintilian, *Institutio Oratoria*, vol. I, I.VII.28—II.X.15

EXERCISES

1. Take a simple sentence like "Tom painted the house today" and render it into one hundred different forms. Stretch your verbal versatility.
    a. "Thomas painted our domicile."
    b. "Tom applied a layer of colored liquid, called paint by most, to the house."
    c. "Tom, wretched vandal, declared his love for Steph beside my front door."
2. Take a longer passage that you admire and paraphrase it without losing its strength. Then take your paraphrase and attempt to translate it back to the original from memory.
3. Find a poem you admire and expand it into prose—retaining its strength (as much as possible).
4. Take five striking phrases from your commonplace book, and try to reuse them in a different context. For example:
    a. "She had just enough brains to make a jaybird fly crooked."
    b. "Henry had just enough brains to wash cars or run for Congress."

REVIEW QUESTIONS

1. What is copiousness? Why is it important for your speaking?
2. What are the two definitions of "commonplace"?
3. What retards copiousness?
4. What are some good ways to achieve copiousness?
5. What is the effect of copiousness on the listener?

Invention

THE FIRST OF THE FIVE CANONS

This is as good a time as any to reveal one of the distinctive features of this book. The reader will discover throughout the chapters that we keep going over some of the same material, and with each pass, we will be treating our subject in greater and greater depth. So with the introduction of the new terms, please make sure you grow to like them, because you will see them again frequently. Many of these terms concern how the subject of rhetoric is divided or arranged.

For example, the five canons of rhetoric (according to the common ancient division) are Invention, Arrangement, Style, Memory, and Delivery. If the speech were a pregnancy, invention would be the conception and delivery would be the . . . delivery. This looks at a speech from its inception to the time when it is given. The divisions here are roughly chronological.

Another method of arranging the study of rhetoric is according to the different parts of the discourse—exordium, narratio, proofs, peroration, and so on. We will be addressing these later in due course.

So first, let us consider invention. According to Señor Cicero, invention was the most important of the five canons. As he put it, "Therefore let us consider what the character of invention should be; this is the most important of all the divisions, and above all is used in every kind of pleading."[1] Before you can say anything, whether poorly or well, you have to come up with something to say. Coming up with the content is called invention.

Now you'll recall that Aristotle's definition of rhetoric gives a high priority to invention—discovering the available means of persuasion.

The speaker, then, should possess the faculties of Invention, Arrangement, Style, Memory, and Delivery. Invention is the devising of matter, true or plausible, that would make the case convincing. Arrangement is the ordering and distribution of the matter, making clear the place to which each thing is to be assigned. Style is the adaptation of suitable words and sentences to the matter devised. Memory is the firm retention in the mind of the matter, words, and arrangement. Delivery is the graceful regulation of voice, countenance, and gesture.

—*Rhetorica Ad Herennium*

---

1. Cicero, *De Inventione*, I.VII.9.

Of the five tasks of the speaker Invention is the most important and the most difficult.
—Rhetorica Ad Herennium

For it is an ordinance of nature that nothing great can be achieved in a moment, and that all the fairest tasks are attended with difficulty, while on births as well she has imposed this law, that the larger the animal, the longer should be the period of gestation.
—**Quintilian**, Institutio Oratoria, vol. 4

Put another way, Aristotle's definition, while inadequate as a definition of rhetoric as a whole, supplies us with an admirable definition of invention. In any given discourse, the speaker is presenting a proposition—any arguable statement that he presents for discussion, a claim which he seeks to advance. He will need to assemble proofs or arguments in support of his proposition. Invention is the process of coming up with those proofs.

There are three kinds of proofs according to Aristotle. He distinguished these three proofs for the "inventor," which are in turn *ethos, pathos*, and *logos*. These three should not be confused with the various specific arguments that might be presented in the course of the talk. All the arguments, and all the aspects of a talk that the audience might find persuasive, can be arranged under the general heads of ethos, pathos, and logos. Ethical proof depends upon the character of the speaker; pathetic proof depends upon an appeal to the emotions of the audience; logical proof depends upon the issues contained within the argument and employs the use of reason and explicit argumentation.

As children of what folks still like to call the Enlightenment, we are very comfortable with the last of these three but very nervous about the first two. Nevertheless, there is still a great deal that can be said for them. Post-enlightenment rhetoric still *uses* ethos and pathos, but likes to pretend that it does not. However, this is hypocritical and breeds confusion. We will talk more about this in subsequent chapters.

Another issue related to invention is the question of what is called stasis theory. We are only going to wave at stasis theory here. For now, stasis theory helps the speaker discover what the fundamental point at issue is. *What are we talking about?* Presumably, understanding what is at issue should help someone formulate arguments. In order to come up with the best arguments, it is necessary to address what the argument is all about in the first place. Learning to do this is what stasis theory is for.

Some of the basics of invention include remembering the importance of copiousness, considering, in some depth, the audience that will be addressed, and the useful exercise (for moderns) of paying more attention than initially is desired to ethos and pathos. In that context, the speaker should consider what specific arguments he will use (logos).

The process of invention begins and ends with several questions. Assuming that the rhetor is settled on his position, he must ask three questions: "Who am I?" "Who are they?" "Where am I trying to get them?" These questions should be asked and answered in terms of ethos, pathos, and logos. Are you a homeschooled kid in a bowtie addressing the local chapter of NOW? Then your discovery should focus on how to (almost impossibly) build ethos. Are you that same kid addressing his assembled proud and loving aunts, uncles, and grandparents? Pathos is obviously in place and ethos won't be much of an issue. Logos is where the action is.

Invention must focus on the problem—an audience is somewhere and they ought to be somewhere else. What are the available means for you (being who you are) to move them? When a student rhetor begins to send real situations and debates into the process of invention—asking and answering those three questions—the value of copiousness should become screamingly apparent.

> It is the first duty of an orator to make himself thoroughly acquainted with the case, a remark which of course applies to all portions of a speech.
> —**Quintilian,** *Institutio Oratoria, vol. 2*

SUGGESTED READING

1. Aristotle, *Rhetoric,* I.VII.I—IX.3I
2. Harry Caplan, ed., *Rhetorica Ad Herennium* (Cambridge: Harvard University Press, 1954), I.I.I—I.XI.18
3. Quintilian, *Institutio Oratoria,* vol. I, II.XI.I—XVIII.5

EXERCISE

1. Choose an argumentative topic and the most hostile (believable) audience that you can. Go through the process of invention with each of the three types of proof (ethos, pathos, logos), listing what you believe would be necessary to move that particular audience. Given who you are, how much of that list is available to you?

REVIEW QUESTIONS

1. What are the five canons of rhetoric? Be prepared to define and discuss each of them.
2. What are the three kinds of proof? Under which canon of rhetoric are they to be studied?
3. Explain why each is legitimately a species of proof.
4. What is stasis theory?
5. What is invention?

LESSON 5

Arrangement

THE SECOND OF THE FIVE CANONS

Arrangement matters a great deal. According to Monsieur Cicero, "when I am collecting arguments for my case I make it my practice not so much to count them as to weigh them."[1] Weighing them is important as part of determining where to put them, which is arrangement.

According to the ancients, arrangement was second in importance only to invention. Once the potential arguments are discovered, it is necessary to arrange them in a manner that is both clear and persuasive. For example, you do not want to present an argument first which depends for its coherence on your third argument. Neither do you want to leave a weak impression with your first argument or attempt to establish ethos in your conclusion, etc.

> This gift of arrangement is to oratory what generalship is to war.
> —**Quintilian,** *Institutio Oratoria, vol. 3*

The basic arrangement of the entire talk looks like this: you have an *exordium*, a *narratio*, proofs, and peroration. The *exordium* is the hook or introduction. The *narratio* is where the salient facts are laid out. The proofs are the place where the explicit arguments for the case are made (and which need to be arranged carefully). The peroration is the conclusion of the speech.

In the *exordium*, you will frequently give the listeners a glimpse of what is to come. What should be revealed (or not) in that glimpse is a matter of arrangement. A speech that begins with "In this talk I intend to prove that . . ." is quite different from "A funny thing happened to my Trans-Am once in Tijuana . . ." Some audiences might want you to get down to business right away. Others might want to be jollied along a bit. In the *narratio*, or (simplistically) the statement of facts, you are setting

> Arrangement is the distribution of things and parts to the places which it is expedient that they should occupy.
> —**Quintilian,** *Institutio Oratoria, vol. 3*

I. *De Oratore*, vol. 2, trans. E. W. Sutton and H. M. Hubbell (Cambridge: Havard University Press, 1942), 309.

out the pieces that you will assemble later. Depending on the complexity of the case, or the brightness of the audience, the *narratio* might give away some of your argumentation. Deciding how that should go is also a matter of arrangement.

A more detailed arrangement would look like this: *exordium, narratio, partitio, (propositio), confirmatio, refutatio,* and *peroratio.* The *exordium* is the introduction, or the front porch of the talk. The *narratio* is where you lay out the facts of the case, collecting the materials you will be using later in the argument. In the *partitio,* the speaker outlines what will follow in the talk. As he does this, he may isolate the *propositio,* which is the point of the speech, the thing to be proven or shown. In the *confirmatio,* the arguments in favor of the *propositio* are marshaled and assembled. In the *refutatio,* the arguments that could be brought against the *propositio* are anticipated and answered. In the *peroratio* we find the concluding remarks.[2] These terms will all be defined in greater detail in a later chapter.

Much of the work in arrangement depends on the nature of the audience. For example, if the audience is hostile, the speaker will need to put a lot more effort into his *exordium* and *refutatio.* If the audience is well-informed, you do not need a lengthy statement of facts in the *narratio*— just enough to let them know that the *speaker* is as well-informed as they are. And if the audience is hostile enough to dispute your facts, then you've chosen the wrong place to fight. You'll never move that mob of scowling faces. Those disputed facts themselves become your goal, your thesis. Flawed arrangement sends you all the way back to the invention phase—you have to assemble something new and swing again.

2. It is worth noting, in this computer age, that Microsoft Word will helpfully turn almost all those Latin words into modern English by adding an "n" to the end of them. You will have to keep a close eye on what you have written.

SUGGESTED READING

I. Quintilian, *Institutio Oratoria*, vol. I, II.XIX.I—III.VI.26

EXERCISE

I. Find a short section (250–500 words) of argumentative prose that
you consider to be compelling, and read aloud publicly. Read as if
your audience dislikes the author and direction of the piece and
you are hoping to sway them. How do you naturally inflect and
gesture differently than you would if the audience were predis-
posed to friendliness?

REVIEW QUESTIONS

I. What is arrangement?
2. What is the basic arrangement of a speech in classical rhetoric?
3. What is the detailed arrangement?
4. What is an *exordium?*
5. What is *partitio?*
6. What is the *propositio?*
7. What is the *narratio?*
8. What is the *refutatio?*
9. What is the *peroratio?*
10. What is *confirmatio?*

LESSON 6

Style

THE THIRD OF THE FIVE CANONS

We have learned that invention and arrangement are very important. Well, so is style. The reader should be discovering by this point that *everything* is important. As Quintilian put it, "without this power [style] all the preliminary accomplishments of rhetoric are as useless as a sword that is kept permanently concealed within its sheath."[1] Brilliantly discovered proofs may be like a coach's inspired game plan, but stilted presentation is a quarterback constantly tripping on his own shoelaces. What's the point of theory? What's the point of ideas, if those ideas are never made flesh? The Greek word for style was *lexis,* meaning "words," while the Latin was *elocutio,* or "speaking out."

Style is not a ham-handed decoration of plain words with other words, which carry the meaning of what you are saying separately from that decoration. Handled rightly, style gives the language more clarity. Style is not the lexical icing for the rhetorical cake—and consider that as a stylistic image. Style is an essential part of the meaning. More than that, style can *be* your meaning. Are we maintaining that the audience should become angry or be appalled by some behavior? Maybe. But what are your rhythms saying? Your word choice? The popping of your syllables? The same is true of any pathos—the style establishes the authority of the content, or it betrays it from the start. But the power of style goes even further. Style can affirm (or give the lie to) propositions as well—even logos depends on it. Would you like to maintain that a classical education better equips students to appreciate truth, goodness, and beauty in the world? Does your own stylistic execution make you a hypocrite? Do you want to talk about the beauty and comfort of the

Style, conceived this way, is something fancy that distracts us from what is essential; it is the varnish that makes the truth at least a little harder to see.
—**Francis-Noel Thomas and Mark Turner,** *Clear and Simple as the Truth*

1. *Institutio Oratoria,* vol. 3, 185.

gospel, but your word choice is entirely harsh? People react to the whole song and rarely to Webster's literal interpretation of the lyrics.

Style is not an afterthought. In other words, style is not achieved by going back over your talk after you have written it in order to put in adjectives. One of the common errors we must resist is thinking that content is one thing and form another. Whether you like it or not, whether your audience realizes it or not, the form—the style—is part of your content.

Elements of style (with apologies to Mssrs. Strunk and White) which you should always consider are the following: The first is correctness. The words used should be in current usage, forsooth!—and you should (for the most part) speak standard English. When you depart from standard usage, it should be deliberate and not an accidental lapse. Like a poet who breaks the rules of poetry for creative effect, this only works when you know and respect the rule you are breaking. If you have never heard of the rules you are breaking, you have no right to do so, and you are likely to come off like a buffoon or a barbarian. Breaking rules, using slang and archaic language can be effective, but it is just as likely to give you an audience busy with wincing.

A second feature should be lucidity, or clarity. Avoid euphemisms, the passive voice, and all the forms of bloviation so popular in our day. Clarity is a function of style, and it is the *first* duty of a speaker to be clear (and to be able to stop talking before being interrupted). When a talk is jargon-laden (integrated, organic, narrative, holistic, synergistic, and—in the hands of posers—classical, Reformed, Trinitarian) to impress the noninitiates, the result is sophistry and not rhetoric. If ordinary people walk away from a talk thinking, "He must be one of those educated boffins," the talk was probably a failure. Exceptions, of course, would be when a technical paper is presented to a technical society, and a layman walks through. But for the most part, the great enemy of style under this heading is every form of humbug, presumption, and posing.

And third, your language should be appropriate to the occasion, the subject, and the audience. You may select (generally) from three levels of style—called (insightfully) by the ancients *grand, middle,* and *plain.* Here are some examples of each.

Clarity renders language plain and intelligible.
—*Rhetorica Ad Herennium*

Archaic words not only enjoy the patronage of distinguished authors, but also give style a certain majesty and charm . . . But such words must be used sparingly and must not thrust themselves upon our notice.
—**Quintilian**, *Institutio Oratoria, vol. 1*

GRAND—Why do the daughters of Zion refuse to dress in a manner which becomes their station?

MIDDLE—Christian young women need to learn the virtue of modesty.

PLAIN—What's with all the bed bait?

It is important that the grand style not be confused with a convoluted or confused style. The virtues of correctness and clarity apply equally to the three levels of style.

A fourth element of style is ornament. Ornament may be divided into two categories—figures of speech and figures of thought. It is here that a speaker will be tempted to go back through in order to "put in some adjectives," but this is a mistake. The eggs of ornament need to be put into the cake mix early on. Adding them too late will only result in a fried (or even raw) egg on top of your birthday cake.

The last element of style to consider is the question of sentence structure, as it relates to the previous questions about the levels of style. The plain style will have shorter sentences and a pithy reliance on basic Anglo Saxon words. The grand style will use sentences that are longer and more intricately arranged.

SUGGESTED READING

1. Quintilian, *Institutio Oratoria*, vol. I, III.VI.27—VIII.17

EXERCISES

1. Find and copy a favorite poem. Edit and expand into prose and then present publicly, attempting to subdue the overt rhythms in your delivery and inflection.

2. Take a simple sentence (like "Ben and Stephanie got married") and rewrite and expand it in several variations, attempting to shift the pathos impact (anger, disgust, amusement, pleasure, etc.) with your stylistic choices.

> There are, then, three kinds of style, called types, to which discourses, if faultless, confines itself: the first we call the Grand; the second, the Middle; the third, the Simple.
> —*Rhetorica Ad Herrennium*

> Those setting out to attain the Middle style, if unsuccessful, stray from the course and arrive at an adjacent type, which we call the Slack because it is without sinews and joints.
> —*Rhetorica Ad Herrennium*

> Those who cannot skilfully employ that elegant simplicity of diction discussed above, arrive at a dry and bloodless kind of style which may aptly be called the Meagre.
> —*Rhetorica Ad Herrennium*

REVIEW QUESTIONS

1. What is style?
2. What are the three levels of style? Give an example of each.
3. What are the five elements of style?

LESSON 7

Memory

THE FOURTH OF THE FIVE CANONS

The next canon of rhetoric is memory. Before talking about this, it is important to get the right metaphor to help us grasp what we are doing. Many modern students have what might be called a "shoebox" view of memory. They think that their brain can only hold so much, and when they get to that point, the shoebox is full (and begins to overflow). But this is to be the victim of a metaphor. The memory is more like a muscle. The more you use it, the more you will be able to do with it— the stronger it becomes. The more you use a shoebox, the less room you'll have later. Some students behave in junior high in such a way as to leave room for something their senior year. But if the memory is more like a muscle, then what they are doing is not "leaving room" but rather allowing an already noodly muscle to atrophy. Someone who runs ten miles a day is not using up his lifetime quota of miles. He is most likely adding to them (assuming, of course, that he looks both ways at crosswalks).

This means that memorization is an activity that is best begun early, and if the student is playing catch-up, the sooner he begins memorizing, the better. He does not accept the "wisdom" of "the sooner you fall behind, the more time you will have to catch up."

To continue the metaphor, it would not be a good idea to try to memorize a mountain of facts the first time out. This would be like trying to run a marathon without having trained at all. Begin simply. Memorize new words, basic Scripture passages, and short poems. This is like walking around the block before you take up jogging, and jogging for six months before you take up really intense running. If a student tries to memorize his whole talk, and that is the first thing he has attempted to memorize, the results will almost certainly be the opposite of encouraging.

If anyone asks me what is the one supreme method of memory, I shall reply, practice and industry.
—**Quintilian,** *Institutio Oratoria, vol. 4*

41

In the modern world, there are many crutches for the memory: Google, iPhones, the entire internet, and yes, books. All of these things can be used to greatly strengthen an already strong mind, or they can prevent strength altogether. They can be armor (and weapons) picked up for particular uses, or they can be like a tower of neck rings on a native woman—weakening the neck within until it is entirely dependent on their support (snapping if they are ever removed). It is easy for contemporary students to devalue memory, trusting in all the readily available AI ("we have technological servants for that"). But that's like a man choosing never to walk because motorized wheel chairs are cheap. We are whatever we are when our servants are removed. Our memories need disciplining especially because of all of our technology, just as walking, running, and exercise have become more necessary with the universality of the car. Did the ancient Romans need trainers to make them walk on treadmills?

That said, Simonides is usually credited with the invention of artificial memory systems. He is the fellow who was behind what you read in the *Rhetorica Ad Herennium*: locate the things you need to memorize in various places with which you are very familiar—a street, house, etc. Mentally tattoo whatever you want to remember onto your brother's forehead, and you'll die before you forget it. When you are memorizing a talk, it is best to memorize the outline of the talk and not the talk verbatim.

A second system of memorization came from a work called *The Dissoiogoi*. The first step is to focus and pay attention. The second step is to practice what is heard, putting it into use. The third is to connect what you want to remember to something you already know. Earth-shaking, yes? Still, it's remarkable how much trouble we appear to have with those three steps. In fact, in America, we're more likely to get a prescription for being distracted before we've tried something as obvious as this.

Aristotle recommended a third memory device, which was to memorize a stock of definitions, along with a stock of premises for use in enthymemes. This will give your memory power out of proportion to what you have memorized. While this may seem bizarre, the principle

If a speech of some length has to be committed to memory, it will be well to learn it piecemeal, since there is nothing so bad for the memory as being overburdened.
—**Quintilian**, *Institutio Oratoria, vol. 4*

applies to becoming a knowledge hound. Be copious. Fill your mind, review the contents of your mind, and fill it somewhere. Learn everything about this world that you possibly can, and work to have it all available to you.

SUGGESTED READING

I. Quintilian, *Institutio Oratoria*, vol. I, III.VIII.18—III.XI.28

EXERCISES

1. Memorize at least five of your commonplaces verbatim. Be able to deliver publicly with citation.
2. Memorize a contemporary, informal poem (no formal meter) of at least twenty-five lines. Be able to deliver it publicly.
3. Compose a short argument (no more than 250 words), memorize, and attempt to deliver publicly without notes.

REVIEW QUESTIONS

1. What is memory?
2. What is the memory device recommended in the *Rhetorica Ad Herennium*?

LESSON 8

Delivery

THE FIFTH OF THE FIVE CANONS

The last of the five canons is delivery. In the ancient world, a much higher priority was given to the spoken word than to the written word. Just imagine today someone presenting their PhD thesis *orally.* This chapter is quite short because a number of the subsequent chapters are actually dedicated to the component parts of delivery—elocution, stance, gestures, eye contact, and so on.

The Greek word for delivery was *hypokrisis,* related to the work of the actor who responded to the chorus in a tragedy. This does not mean that delivery is acting. As Cicero maintained, there is a difference between acting in a fictional situation and acting in a real situation.

In vocal delivery, pay attention (*a la* Aristotle) to voice, pitch, and rhythm. Memorization is important here—as you are recalling the various elements of your talk, the audience should not be able to smell the wood burning. One of the most important things you can do with your voice is to have it sound natural, and in order for this to happen, it is important not to be doing two or three others things. If you are desperately trying to remember what the next point is, or you are wondering about the subject/verb agreement in the sentence that flew from your mouth three seconds ago, then it will be terribly difficult to sound natural. You won't sound natural because it won't *be* natural.

Another important area to note is gesture. The most important gesture is what you do with your head and eyes. One of the best things to do in this regard is to take note of some of your most common and natural gestures (the sort of thing you do in ordinary conversation), and then employ a disciplined form of that same gesture in a talk. Other than that, gesticulation is not nearly as important now as it was in the ancient world.

> We must aim at speaking as well as we can, but must not try to speak better than our nature will permit.
> —**Quintilian,** *Institutio Oratoria, vol. 4*

To work on delivery, memorize a short passage you admire and practice reciting it aloud whenever you can. Give stirring orations to the windshield of your car during those long commutes. It doesn't matter what the driver of the car next to you thinks.

SUGGESTED READING

1. Aristotle, *Rhetoric*, I.IX.32—XI.4
2. *Rhetorica Ad Herennium*, I.XI.19—I.XVII.27
3. Quintilian, *Institutio Oratoria*, vol. 2, IV.Preface.I—II.35

EXERCISE

1. Find a short selection (200–250 words) and attempt to shift the tone of the piece with your delivery. Angry becomes funny, funny becomes sad, sad becomes angry, etc. Do not fear failure. To some extent, it's inevitable.

REVIEW QUESTIONS

1. What is delivery?
2. What is the Greek term for it?
3. According to Aristotle, what are the three important elements of your vocal delivery?
4. What is the other important aspect of delivery?

Ethos

The categories of proof we have already mentioned are *ethos, pathos,* and *logos.* We will be spending a good amount of space on logos (that is, on argumentation), so a little more attention given to ethos here will do no harm. Ethos and pathos are greatly neglected and disparaged in our day. It is assumed that they are what make sophistry wrong, and that what we should strive for is a talk or composition that is a masterpiece of logical perfection, delivered with all the energy of a computer printout. But this is seriously misguided.

Quintilian describes the impact of ethos in this way, "As regards the orator, the qualities which will most commend him are courtesy, kindliness, moderation and benevolence." He goes on to qualify this, saying that sometimes the opposite qualities are what is needed. A good man hates what is wicked, and this severity should sometimes be in evidence. But most of the time, in ordinary discourse, the qualities which need to be cultivated most are those mentioned above. They need to be cultivated, and they need to be *visible.* They are an essential part of what makes a talk compelling (or not).

Ethos refers to those proofs that rely upon the orator's character, personality, or reputation—they depend on trust and on becoming trustworthy. The ancients did not shy away from talking about this directly (with regard to their own virtues), but the influence of Christianity has thankfully put an end to that. In other words, it is not possible today to boost one's ethos by spending a good portion of the speech talking about how humble one is. But this has not made the question of ethos disappear. Neither has it diminished the importance of it.

Disciplining oneself and cultivating a compelling ethos is not an easy matter. For Christians, it should be considered as integral with the process

A good man will see that everything he says is consistent with his dignity and the respectability of his character; for we pay too dear for the laugh if we raise it, it is at the cost of our own integrity.
—**Quintilian,** *Institutio Oratoria, vol. 2*

of sanctification. It is *not* learning how to be a hypocrite. Character is manifested in community, and this means that the rhetorical questions concerning ethos are matters of love. In some ways, the Christian should do good deeds in a way that is not for public display (Mt. 6:3). However, in another sense, we are not to have what we do hidden away (Mt. 5:14–16). And when we serve the Father in secret, He promises to reward us *openly* (Mt. 6:4). To put it all together, a speaker should be aware of the reputation he has and he should use it in his talk—either leaning into it or away from it—and he needs to do this without showboating.

On the question of ethos, we have a general difference between Aristotle and Quintilian. Aristotle distinguished between invented and situated ethos. Invented ethos is where the speaker "invents" his ethos for a particular rhetorical occasion. Situated ethos is where the speaker already has a good reputation that he can use. But in this, remember Quintilian's definition of rhetoric—a man must genuinely be good and not just have the appearance of it.

Invented ethos is not the same thing as hypocrisy, but it does lend itself to hypocrisy more readily. Invented ethos is what a speaker must develop going into a situation cold—as when someone is speaking at a conference where no one there has met him before. His audience doesn't know him from Adam's house cat, and consequently, invented ethos must be made evident during the course of the talk (past experiences, sources consulted, even vocal intonation and bizarrely twitching eyelids contribute to invented ethos). Aristotle said three things must be in evidence—practical wisdom, virtue, and good will. For example, both of us have been introduced to audiences in strange cities by very nice men apparently intent on preemptively destroying any and all useful ethos through weird, inflated, and excessive praise. All of that type of thing must be undone immediately and without insulting the unfortunate emcee. Self-deprecating jokes can become your best friend, and using them to diffuse a bad introduction is an example of quickly invented ethos. Something needs to be done to reveal the speaker's character—likes and dislikes, self-perception, and so on—and it needs to be done within the opening minutes. An abusive form of invented ethos would be politicians who develop a Southern accent when they are stumping for votes in Arkansas.

For we have come to regard direct and natural speech as incompatible with genius, while all that is in any way abnormal is admired as exquisite.

—**Quintilian,** *Institutio Oratoria, vol. 1*

Aristotle, the Greek, made more distinctions here than did Quintilian, the Roman. Part of the problem may have been that the Latin language did not really have an adequate term for ethos (their term for it was _persona_, which meant mask). This reveals the problem that we face—adopting a persona can be hypocritical. But it is always necessary to reveal one's persona.

Some of the common problems with ethos reveal why the subject is so important to anyone who wants to be effective in their public speaking.

Shrillness—this is the standard ethos problem among Christians and conservatives in the culture wars. This problem is so common that it would be easy to assume that someone is out there somewhere teaching people how to do this. "When you write a letter to the editor about abortion, make sure it looks like it was written with a fisted crayon and that the paper it is written on is spittle-flecked." Those who succumb to the temptation to be shrill may defend themselves by saying that the issue they are addressing is too important to waste time on rhetorical considerations. But their reasoning should be just the reverse of this. Because poor ethos makes people ignore what is being said, the more important a subject is, the more important it is to cultivate a strong ethos.

Discourtesy—a speaker should not only like his audience, he should also have taken some trouble on their behalf. Having an affection for an audience is not the same thing as avoiding a dislike for them. Taking trouble for others is not the same as not giving trouble to others. It is the responsibility of the speaker, the one who has the floor, to maintain a genuine courtesy toward those who are listening to him. When such courtesies are visible, as they should be, the auditors will want to reciprocate.

Slovenliness—this might be considered a subset of the previous category, or one application of it. Modern Americans do not like being told how to dress, but that is too bad. One way to show contempt for an audience is to dress in a manner that suits only yourself. We like to think that we dress for comfort and not for "appearances." But a better way of thinking about it is to compare the difference between dressing for the comfort of the wearer and the comfort of the viewer. A speaker should establish or reinforce his ethos through how he dresses. This can be ridiculed as "dress for success," but most problems in that area

> For the orator who gives the impression of being a bad man while he is speaking, is actually speaking badly.
> —**Quintilian,** _Institutio Oratoria, vol. 2_

> An impudent, disorderly, or angry tone is always unseemly.
> —**Quintilian,** _Institutio Oratoria, vol. 4_

are not the result of attempting it but rather of attempting it in a ham-handed way. And, to be frank, most of the problems in this area do not come in the area of overdressing. They come in the area of piercings and tattoos and ratty jeans. Lose them. Rise above the conformity of industrialized American edginess and comfort.

Ignorance—this is the problem of not doing the necessary homework before speaking on a subject that requires homework to be done. It is very important for a speaker to be well-informed about the issue at hand. If a speaker is simply ignorant, that is more a problem with logos, with his argumentation. If a speaker is ignorant when he has the ability to be informed, but did not take the trouble, then that is a problem with ethos. His ignorance is an insult to his listeners—"I could not be troubled to inform myself on this subject before making you listen to me talk about it." It is offered as an insult and is frequently taken as one.

Establishing invented ethos in the course of a talk can obviously be a tricky business. The speaker must think through how he might reveal his ethos without bragging. "I have read a pile of books and know what I am talking about" is a clunky attempt to establish ethos and actually wrecks it. "As Eric Hoffer once argued . . ." is a subtle way to indicate that the speaker is well-read and is not just making his speech up as he goes along.

Think about how to establish good will with your audience.

Another issue has to do with settling on a "rhetorical voice." A choice of voice determines what is called "rhetorical distance." This metaphor refers to how close or far away an audience feels from the speaker and includes much more than just the physical distance—although physical distance does affect rhetorical distance, and all of it affects ethos.

The one speaking must ask what distance is appropriate to the situation. Ask again: Who am I? Who are they? Where am I trying to get them? You should know what role distance might play in your speech, and you should know what increases or decreases that distance. Formality increases distance. Strong attitude decreases distance, while ambivalence maintains distance. Voice is governed by many stylistic considerations, most notably grammatical person (I, you, we, they, it), verb tense, active or passive voice, the size of words, and various qualifiers. The

Confidence often labours under the disadvantage of being regarded as arrogance. But there are certain tricks for acquiring goodwill, which though almost universal, are by no means to be neglected, if only to prevent their being first employed against ourselves.

—**Quintilian,** *Institutio Oratoria, vol. 2*

points made below are by no means exhaustive but are given simply to illustrate how questions of voice and distance operate.

Person—there are many things to consider here. "I" can seem egotistical and therefore can increase distance. But done well, it can also seem intimate and chummy. "You" can have all the strengths and weaknesses of dogmatism and a pointed finger. Third person creates the greatest formality and distance, at least usually.

Tense—the present tense is more immediate and decreases distance.

Active and Passive—the active voice tends to decrease distance. The passive voice is a good way to make it sound like no one in particular is responsible for anything, and yet, even so, it can be acknowledged, forthrightly, that mistakes were made—by somebody.

Big Words—such polysyllabic words affect voice and distance. Using such words tends to reveal the speaker as well-educated, and such words are generally more precise. However they also increase formality and distance. One thing to do here is try to have it both ways (utilizing both grand and plain styles to undercut the distance impact of the big word)—"He chased his epistemology around like a little, greased pig."

Qualifiers—words like some, most, virtually, and so forth decrease distance between speaker and audience.

Now if we bring this back to situated ethos, and the Christian understanding of character, we can see how the two can relate to one another. The one working on such characteristics of invented character (as a means of discipline) is developing what will become part of his situated ethos, or standing character.

> Let no one however demand from me a rigid code of rules such as most authors of textbooks have laid down . . . If the whole of rhetoric could be thus embodied in one compact code, it would be an easy task of little compass: but most rules are liable to be altered by the nature of the case, circumstances of time and place, and by hard necessity itself.
> —**Quintilian,** *Institutio Oratoria, vol. 1*

SUGGESTED READING

1. Aristotle, *Rhetoric,* I.XI.5—XII.10
2. Quintilian, *Institutio Oratoria,* vol. 2, IV.II—36-III.16

EXERCISE

1. Choose something you believe to be worthy of praise (school of architecture, sport, film, person, etc.) and a hypothetical audience extremely hostile to your selection. Write a short epideictic piece (300–350 words) revealing all that is wonderful about what you've chosen. Attempt to soften the audience's hostility by carefully building your own invented ethos, as well as the secondary ethos of that which you are praising. Present publicly and collect objective criticism about your success or failure.

REVIEW QUESTIONS

1. According to Quintilian, what are the four characteristics which are important for ethos?
2. What is the difference between invented ethos and situated ethos?
3. Which one lends itself more readily to a situation where the speaker is coming from out of town and is new to the audience?
4. What is rhetorical distance?
5. What does grammatical voice do to distance?
6. What does formality do to distance?
7. What does verb tense do to distance?
8. What do the active and passive voice do to it?
9. What do qualifiers do to distance?
10. What do polysyllabic words do to distance?

Pathos

Now, on to *pathos*, the one "proof" that we as moderns are all the most nervous about.

First, this is as good a place as any to kick against our assumptions about the nature of proof. How can we call ethos (credibility and trustworthiness) a proof, let alone pathos (appeals to emotion)? We are all good little spawning salmon of the Enlightenment, surely we know that only science and formal logic can talk about "proof." Right? Wrong. In fact, as Cicero might have put it, wrongedy-wrong-wrong.

What does it mean to prove something? In this day and age, our minds immediately drift toward the establishment of certainty. Beyond not just a reasonable doubt, but any shadow of a doubt. But we are finite beings. We can never come to inerrant certainty about anything using only the little mechanical tools within our own brains. We must have faith. We have faith in our five senses, in our observations, in the observations of others, in the "laws" of logic, and in our own mutant concept of "proof." Faith is great, when acknowledged and ultimately rooted in that which is faithworthy—God, the infinite Creator, the One who is not out to deceive but to reveal. That is why we can trust our own eyes (because He made them) and the patterns of nature and logic (because He made them too—they are outworkings of His own consistent and unchanging character). That is why (when healthy cynicism has been satisfied) we can even trust each other.

To prove something does not mean "to convince." That is simple manipulation and sophistry. To prove something does not mean "to objectively establish something as true beyond a shadow of a doubt." That isn't possible for us. To prove something is "to obligate belief." The goal is to reveal something as true, and to do so in a way that resonates

53

with the secondary witnesses of the consciences of your audience. They can turn away from it if they like (as they often did from Christ and His apostles), but they have seen, and they have been obligated. Once truth has been glimpsed, the conscience has been bound. And truth can be seen through the declaration of a strong authority (ethos) and the secondary witness of the emotions (pathos). Emotions (when in their proper place) have their own legitimate authority. Think about the abortion discussion, or an appeal to a man guilty of beating his wife, or someone walking out of a marriage, etc. Guilt and sorrow can speak truth in those cases. When appealing to a third party to intervene, anger can also be legitimate. Every emotion has an appropriate and authoritative voice somewhere.

Incidentally, the above definition of "proof" is why rhetors should be cautious when claiming to have "proved" anything. What you are saying is that all who have heard must now believe or be guilty of consciously turning away from the truth. That says a great deal not only of your logic, but of your ability in clear and concise communication. If you are maintaining that doughnuts are superior to cinnamon rolls, then save the big claims for a less subjective area. Simply convincing an audience is sufficient in that case, though the types of "proof" are still in play. You aren't able to bind (nor should you want to bind) anyone's conscience about such a petty issue. Save "obligated belief" for the bigger more substantive brawls.

Moving into pathos specifically, we first must shake our common notion of what "that's pathetic" means. Other words in English will help us with this. Compare your own (pathos) response to these two sentences: "His oration manipulated their emotions like a master puppeteer" and "His oration successfully evoked a deep sympathy." The word sympathy comes from *pathos*. We are rationalists if we think that every appeal to the emotions is necessarily dishonest, because there are times when it is dishonest not to appeal to them.

On this subject, we need to learn to distinguish without separating. We can make a distinction between the mind and the affections because Scripture does. This distinction is made in every Bible passage that speaks about "the heart and the reins." Our metaphor for the same thing is "the head and heart." Scripture recognizes the distinction between that which is cognitively known and that which is viscerally felt. However, there is a difference between making a distinction and achieving a separation. We can distinguish height and depth, but we cannot separate them. (Erase height, and you've erased depth. Erase depth, and the height is gone as well.) In the biblical worldview, the head and heart go together. An absence of one destroys the other.

So here we must make a crucial distinction. Our emotions are *not* to be subject to our reason. (Did you catch that?) This is a Hellenistic way of proceeding, and once this dichotomy is set up, people "pays their money and they takes their choice." In other words, people careen between an Apollonian (rationalistic) view of the world and a Dionysian (subjectivist) view of the world. For an example of this, compare the neo-classical era and the romantic era. In recent history, compare the late fifties and the late sixties. The common assumption is that if reason does not rule the emotions, then nothing will. This supposition is often supported by the emotional among us, who proceed in the most nonlinear fashion imaginable (giving emotions a rather tarnished reputation).

Our emotions cannot be autonomous, but neither can our reason be. And we do not escape from the trap by subjecting one to the other. Rather, both must be subject to the authority of Scripture. This means that the rule to have in pathetic proofs is a scriptural rule and not a rational rule. This means the question is whether it is *scriptural* to feel a certain way and not whether it is *rational* to feel that way.

In turn, this means that emotional manipulations are excluded but not for the reason we have usually assumed they should be. Lousy rock bands use a lot of lasers and dry ice. In the same way, lousy rhetors haul in sentimental and weepy stories about the dying puppy's last wish. Yet this does not mean that we should banish sentiment, or weeping. Tears displacing thought is objectionable, when thought was called for, but similarly, thought instead of tears is objectionable, when tears were called for.

Take this back to the classical world. Aristotle and Cicero discussed emotions in sets: anger and calm, love and hate, fear and confidence, shame and shamelessness, compassion or pity and indignation, envy and

The Appeal to Pity must be brief, for nothing dries more quickly than a tear.
—*Rhetorica Ad Herennium*

emulation, and so forth. In some ways, this can be helpful but always beware of the assumptions. Virtue in the Christian sense is not a matter of "splitting the difference" between "self-evident" extremes and is not a matter of following the golden mean. Virtue means loving God with all one's heart, soul, mind, and strength, and that is not found by splitting the difference.

When considering what kind of pathos to employ, it is again important to remember the nature of the audience (and their view of you—ethos). For example, younger audiences are more impetuous, while older audiences are more suspicious. This means that a flamboyant appeal is less likely to be helpful to an older audience. Audiences, generally speaking, are either hostile, indifferent, or receptive. The degree of pathos must vary accordingly.

As a speaker composes his pathos, he must first feel what he would evoke. In doing this, he paints a vivid scene—an *enargeia*. And as a Christian, you must feel it honestly, which is of course quite different from honestly feeling it. Honesty at this point is not a matter of spontaneity; it is a question of correspondence—does the feeling line up with the logos and the ethos. Is it consistent with them? The issue is whether the speaker feels what he does honestly and not whether he simply appears to feel it.

Second, in developing pathos, it is important to use honorific or pejorative words. Honorific words are words of praise, and pejorative terms are terms of abuse. For example, take a simple sentence, which is mostly indifferent, and turn it either direction.

1. Tom went downtown, and all afternoon he spent his energy and time looking for a set of golf clubs.

2. Tom, excellent fellow, went downtown and spent the whole stinking afternoon wasting his energy and time (not that it was that great a loss), looking for a set of idiot clubs. Needless to say, he found them.

3. Tom, always thoughtful, went downtown and gave up his day to find the ideal set of golf clubs for his father. They were the perfect Christmas gift.

The prime essential for stirring the emotions of others is, in my opinion, first to feel those emotions oneself.
—**Quintilian,** *Institutio Oratoria, vol. 2*

SUGGESTED READING

1. Aristotle, *Rhetoric,* I.XII.11—XIII.19
2. Quintilian, *Institutio Oratoria,* vol. 2, IV.IV.1—V.IX.16

EXERCISE

1. Write a short narrative paragraph (100 words) aiming for a particular audience sympathies. Write two different versions of the same paragraph attempting to relocate sympathies. Deliver all three publicly (back-to-back).

REVIEW QUESTIONS

1. What does it mean to prove something?
2. What distinguishes a right use of pathos from simple manipulation?
3. What must we distinguish without separating?
4. What should the relationship between thought and tears be?
5. In what ways does the average age of the audience matter?

LESSON 11

The Basics of Reasoning

The fact that we are spending several chapters on logos does not mean that ethos and pathos can be dismissed as unimportant. But it does mean that the logos can be hard to master, and, more importantly, it is easy for confused or dishonest people to twist and distort. All that glitters is not rationality.

For those who have taken some logic, there may be redundancies here, but the crossroads of formal logic and formal rhetoric is an important one. Review is always helpful, and to omit this discussion would leave a gaping hole in this text, and in any young rhetor's training.

As we proceed, some basic laws of reasoning must be kept in mind. First, consider the law of the excluded middle. This means that there is no middle ground between true or false. Second, remember the law of identity. This means that if a statement is true, then it is true. And last, tenaciously hold onto the law of noncontradiction. This means that a statement cannot be both true and false. These three laws may be summed up by saying that there is no third way, truth is truth, and truth excludes falsity. It is important for us as Christians to note that these are not laws that God must "obey" but rather are laws that we can describe as reflective of His nature and character. These laws of logic are descriptive of the way He is. We could not reject any of them without opening the door to the worst heresies imaginable.

Think of logic as the bedrock for logos. Logic deals with statements and their relationships to one another. A statement is a particular kind of sentence. Not all sentences are statements (i.e., questions, commands, or babbling). A statement is a sentence which can be said to be either true or false without contradiction.

Almost all others who have written on the art of oratory have started with the assumption that their readers were perfect in all other branches of education and that their own task was merely to put the finishing touches to their rhetorical training.
—**Quintilian**, *Institutio Oratoria, vol. 1*

In the practice of logic, statements serve either as conclusions or premises. In a chain of arguments, a statement can serve as both a conclusion in one argument and a premise in the next. The conclusion is what you are seeking to prove, and the premises are the reasons for coming to that conclusion.

Argumentation that is twisted in some fashion is called a fallacy. The twisting has reference to what the argument is attempting or claiming to do. For our purposes here, there are two kinds of fallacies—fallacies of form and fallacies of distraction. A fallacy of form occurs when the structure of the argument is wrong. It is therefore wrong regardless of what nouns might be dropped into that structure. A fallacy of distraction occurs when the structure of argument is being ignored, shifted, or insulted in some way. Many student logicians unfortunately begin to treat fallacies of distraction as if they were fallacies of form. They identify the structure of a particular attack (a personal attack, for example) and conclude that it must be fallacious when it may or may not be. Fallacies of distraction are never fallacious by structure or mechanism but become fallacies when they are (drumroll, please) distracting from the central issues at hand.

We must also distinguish between deductive and inductive arguments. A deductive argument is either valid or invalid (with regard to form), and the conclusion is true or false. Validity means that the truth of the premises would necessarily imply the truth of the conclusion. An inductive argument has a conclusion that is either true or false but, with regard to its structure, is considered to be either strong or weak, not valid or invalid. (This is because every inductive argument would be invalid by definition, making the classification useless). A deductive argument moves from the general to the particular. An inductive argument moves from the particular to the general. Consequently, it gets you farther, but there is more room for problems to creep in.

For example, a deductive argument says that all crows are black. This bird here is a crow. Therefore, this bird is black. As deductive arguments go, this is ironclad. By contrast, an inductive argument says that "I saw a crow once. It was black. Therefore all crows must be black." This argument is reasoning from one crow to all crows, going from the particular to the general, and it is weak. But another inductive argument can be strong, saying that "I am getting my doctorate in crows. I have seen 123,000 of them on five continents. They were all black. My argument is that the rest of them are black too." This has the same structural form as the first one-crow argument, but this inductive argument is stronger. The sample size is reasonable given the sweeping nature of the conclusion.

So armed, let us turn to discuss fallacies of form and go back to our earlier crow argument. Suppose we were to argue that "All crows are black. This thing here is black. Therefore it must be a crow." This argument has a fallacious form, and it will always have that flawed form regardless of what nouns are substituted in for *crows* and *black*. All cows give milk. This animal gives milk. Therefore it is a cow. (Incidentally, this particular fallacy is called affirming the consequent, and you'll learn more about it later—if it isn't a close personal friend of yours already.). The argument basically says, "If P, then Q. Q. Therefore, P." Because it is a fallacy, the appropriate exhortation here would be: Stop it. Don't do that.

> There are many things which are true, but scarcely credible, just as there are many things which are plausible though false.
> —**Quintilian,** *Institutio Oratoria, vol. 2*

Fallacies of distraction work in another way. This kind of error is far more common during informal argumentation, and this is where we will spend a great deal of our time. Suppose a man is losing an argument, and so he responds with some version of "Look! A comet!" or, "You, my friend, are committing a hate crime." Or "Don't you love the children?" These are fallacies because of how they are being employed, because of the narrative context and the obvious intent to change the subject while losing an argument. If there really is a comet worth noticing, then it is no longer a fallacy.

SUGGESTED READING

1. Aristotle, *Rhetoric,* I.XIV.I—XV.26
2. Quintilian, *Institutio Oratoria,* vol. 2, V.X.I—X.109

EXERCISE

I. Construct a short argumentative composition (300 words), developing at least one deductive and one inductive argument.

REVIEW QUESTIONS

1. What is the law of the excluded middle?
2. What is the law of identity?
3. What is the law of noncontradiction?
4. What is a fallacy?
5. What is the difference between deductive and inductive arguments?
6. What is a fallacy of form?
7. What is a fallacy of distraction?

The Structure of Argument

The subject before us now is the square of opposition, which will bring us, in due time, to the categorical syllogism. We are beginning our analysis of the structure of argument, and the square of opposition should simply be understood as a tool to help conceptualize the relationships between various kinds of statements. As should be evident by now, an argument is basically a certain arrangement of statements. The square of opposition provides us with a quick way of identifying possible problems in arguments.

The way we set this up is first to translate all indicative statements (statements which must either be true or false) into statements using the linking verb *is*. This tends to awkwardness and syntax like a clunky fair, but it does make the analysis easier later on.

Example: "Paul's epistles exhibit great depth of feeling" turns into "All Paul's epistles are great depth of feeling exhibitors." This in turn becomes "All P are Q," with P standing in for Paul's epistles and Q standing in for feeling indicators.

Such statements can be affirmative or negative, and they can be universal or particular. This gives us four possible combinations—the four corners of our square.

The terms in the statement (the Ps and Qs) can either be distributed or undistributed. This refers to whether or not the statement is being made of every member of the class. In the statement "All triangles are three-sided figures," the term triangles is distributed. The claim refers to every last one of them. In the statement "Rainy days are melancholy," the term "rainy days" is not intended to be distributed—although someone could take it that way. "Are you saying that *every last* rainy day is this way?"

Wisdom is intelligence capable, by a certain judicious method, of distinguishing good and bad.
—*Rhetorica Ad Herennium*

Taking the definitions above, we now have four kinds of statement we need to arrange.

Universal affirmative—All P are Q.
 We call this an A statement.
Universal negative—No P are Q.
 We call this an E statement.
Particular affirmative—Some P are Q.
 We call this an I statement.
Particular negative—Some P are not Q.
 We call this an O statement.

Now, what about distribution? Glad you asked.

	SUBJECT	PREDICATE
A statement	distributed	undistributed
E statement	distributed	distributed
I statement	undistributed	undistributed
O statement	undistributed	distributed

We arrange them thus, one statement for each corner of the square:

A statement   E statement

I statement   O statement

Note that universality is sitting on the top and particularity on the bottom. Positivity (friend of man and beast) is on the left and negativity (friendless and lonely) is on the right. These different kinds of statements have predictable relationships with one another, and every statement of a particular kind has that same relationship to every statement of another particular kind.

A and E: These are contraries. This means they cannot both be true, but they can both be false. They are not contradictions!

A and O: These are contradictories. They cannot both be true, and they cannot both be false. True contradiction!

E and I: These are also contradictories. They cannot both be true, and they cannot both be false.

I and O: These are subcontraries. They can both be true, but they cannot both be false.

A to I: This is subimplication. The truth of A requires the truth of I.

E to O: This is subimplication. The truth of E requires the truth of O.

I to A: This is superimplication. This is an implication of falsity. If the particular is false, the universal must be also.

O to E: This is superimplication. This is an implication of falsity. If the particular is false, the universal must be also.

When it comes to distinguishing between sub- and superimplications: falsity floats, truth runs downhill.

SUGGESTED READING

1. Aristotle, *Rhetoric*, I.XV.27—II.II.10
2. Quintilian, *Institutio Oratoria*, vol. 2, V.X.110—XIII.33

EXERCISE

1. Be able to draw a diagram of the square of opposition from memory. Label and describe each relationship. Assert truth or falsity of one corner and unpack what can be concluded about the truth or falsity of the others.

REVIEW QUESTIONS

1. What is a statement?
2. What is a conclusion?
3. What is a premise?
4. What is a fallacy?
5. What is a fallacy of form?
6. What is a fallacy of distraction?
7. What is a deductive argument?
8. What is an inductive argument?
9. What is a valid argument?
10. What is an invalid argument?
11. What is a strong or weak argument?
12. What is the law of the excluded middle?
13. What is the law of identity?
14. What is the law of noncontradiction?
15. What is the square of opposition?
16. What is a universal affirmative?
17. What is an A statement?
18. What is a universal negative?
19. What is an E statement?
20. What is a particular affirmative?
21. What is an I statement?
22. What is a particular negative?
23. What is an O statement?
24. What is a distributed term?
25. What is an undistributed term?
26. What is a contrary relationship?
27. What is a contradictory relationship
28. What is subcontrariety?
29. What is subimplication?
30. What is superimplication?

Syllogisms

CATEGORICAL AND HYPOTHETICAL

L et us jump right in. A categorical syllogism follows this pattern:

All P are Q.
Some Q are R.
Therefore, some R are P.

This is a deductive argument, and it is therefore either invalid or valid.

But before deciding which, we need to get some terms straight in our minds. This type of syllogism contains three statements: the first two of them are premises, and the third is the conclusion. It also contains three terms. The predicate term of the conclusion is called the major term. In this case, the major term is P. The minor term is the subject term of the conclusion. That means R is the minor term. The middle term is that which is in both premises but not in the conclusion. The middle term is that which connects both premises together. It is the mutual friend of the major and minor terms, and they only relate to one another through it.

The major premise is the premise which contains the major term. In this case, it is the first premise. But note carefully, the major premise is not necessarily the one that comes first. The minor premise contains the minor term, and here it is the second premise. There is no such thing as a middle premise, so don't go writing that on any quizzes.

There are different ways to test for validity, but we are going to concentrate on testing by rule. It is important to know that testing by rule only gives the argument's validity. If an argument is valid but wrong, we would say it is unsound. If it is both valid and true, we say that it is sound.

Now we must consider mood and figure. The mood of a categorical syllogism is simply an abbreviation of how the argument looks in the categories created by the square of opposition. Our argument here would be called an AII. This means it is an A statement, followed by an I statement, concluded with an I.

The term *figure* refers to the arrangement of the middle term in the argument. Remember that the middle term only occurs in the premises.

> Figure 1—when the middle term is the subject of the major premise and predicate of the minor.
> Figure 2—when the middle term is the predicate of the major premise and predicate of the minor.
> Figure 3—when the middle term is the subject of the major premise and subject of the minor.
> Figure 4—when the middle term is the predicate of the major premise and subject of the minor.

Bring it all together, and our argument can be summarized as an AII-4.

There are five rules for testing validity here. If any of the rules are violated, the syllogism is invalid. The rules are as follows:

1. In at least one premise, the middle term must be distributed.

2. If a term is distributed in the conclusion, it must also be distributed in its premise.

3. A valid syllogism cannot have two negative premises.

4. A valid syllogism cannot have a negative premise and affirmative conclusion.

5. A valid syllogism cannot have two affirmative premises and a negative conclusion.

Mixed hypothetical syllogisms follow a different pattern. There are four possible combinations, two of them valid, and two invalid. First, let's consider the invalid ones.

> I. If P, then Q.
> Q.
> Therefore P.

This is called the fallacy of *affirming the consequent*. It is the bread and butter of fuzzy thinkers everywhere.

2. If P, then Q.
   Not P.
   Therefore not Q.
This is called the fallacy of *denying the antecedent*.

Now, the valid forms:

3. If P, then Q.
   P.
   Therefore Q.
This is called *modus ponens*, which means "the way of affirming."

4. If P, then Q.
   Not Q.
   Therefore not P.
This is called *modus tollens*, "the way of denying."

A great deal more can be done with hypothetical syllogisms in the study of formal logic, but in the context of a rhetoric text, these four familiar basics are sufficient (and necessary).

What has been presented in these few chapters are the bare rudiments of symbolic logic. For further study, please consult *Introductory Logic*.[1] There are many other avenues down which a man could pursue these issues, and many other truth trees up which he could bark profitably. But the point here has been only to give the basics, which is all that is necessary in most day-to-day argumentation.

Many, however, in their passionate desire to win a reputation for eloquence are content to produce showy passages which contribute nothing to the proof of their case.
—**Quintilian,** *Institutio Oratoria, vol. 3*

I. James B. Nance and Douglas J. Wilson, *Introductory Logic for Christian & Home Schools* (Moscow: Canon Press, 2006).

SUGGESTED READING

1. Aristotle, *Rhetoric*, II.II.II—IV.12
2. Quintilian, *Institutio Oratoria*, vol. 2, V.XIII.34—VI.I.26

EXERCISE

1. Compose a short humorous and argumentative piece (300–500 words). Develop one primary hypothetical syllogism, then establish the truth of the premises. Present publicly.

REVIEW QUESTIONS

1. What is a categorical syllogism?
2. What is a major term?
3. What is a middle term?
4. What is a minor term?
5. What is a major premise?
6. What is a minor premise?
7. What is a sound argument?
8. What is an unsound argument?
9. What is the mood of an argument?
10. What is a figure in an argument?
11. What are the five rules of validity?
12. What is the fallacy of affirming the consequent?
13. What is a fallacy of denying the antecedent?
14. What is *modus ponens?*
15. What is a *modus tollens?*

Fallacies
on the Street I

Normally, the formal logic of the preceding chapters takes up at least a semester of study. The point of the introduction here was to acquaint (or reacquaint) you with the basic terminology. But in most debates that a public speaker might find himself in, the comeback will rarely be something like, "Hey! That was an IEA-3!" The point here is to learn how to shape logic in ordinary language and how to answer common mistakes of logic in ordinary language. So in learning "street-fighting" logic, the first thing to do (as always) is to make some distinctions. We find three types of fallacies: fallacies of distraction, of ambiguity, and of form. We are no longer doing logic in the realm of Euclid, as above, and so you should soon notice that fallacies of ambiguity could also, if we wanted them to, be considered distracting.

We must also note these are only fallacies depending upon how they are used. In other words, it is possible to reason rightly while using some of these arguments. Some purists want to consider them fallacies in each and every situation, but human reasoning, when it is on the wing, takes much of its meaning from the context. This means they cannot be handled as though they were contextless. They are fallacies when they are (uncalled for) distractions or deceptions.

Initially, we will consider some of the fallacies of distraction.

First, the *ipse dixit* fallacy. This is Latin for "he has said it himself." As always, there are wheels within hermeneutical wheels. The fallacy is committed when an illegitimate appeal is made to authority. The form this takes is this: "X says thus and such. Thus and such must be the case." Or, "If P says it, then Q must be. P does in fact say it. Therefore Q and, incidentally, Q.E.D."

This is *modus ponens* and is therefore valid. But how can it be valid and a fallacy? Hey? Remember, this is street logic. The issue is the legitimacy of the appeal not the structure. If the authority is legitimate (and relevant), then there is no fallacy at all. If not, then *ipse dixit.*

Not *ipse dixit*: "The Constitution says that each state can only have two senators, and therefore, each state can only have two senators."

Ipse dixit: "Harry Peters says that we should have three senators each, and therefore, we should have three senators."

Now, the *ad populum* fallacy. This fallacy means an appeal to the masses. The thing which makes it a fallacy is that the appeal is made to the mere mass of the masses (to their massness qua massness—ooh, that's fun to say) and not to those aspects of man which the masses have, which are legitimate to appeal to (consciences, for example). Remember that ethos and pathos and logos are to be balanced and not substituted for one another because one or more element is AWOL. When such an imbalanced appeal is made, the fallacy is committed.

Not *ad populum:* "How can anyone fail to be moved by such a story?"

Ad populum: "How can anyone fail to be moved by such a story?"

Dig into the context.

The *ad baculum* fallacy is an appeal "to the stick." Once again, we find that we do not have a level playing field, which is a drag for modern man, because he is an egalitarian and really likes to have a level playing field. The Scriptures tell us that the rod is for the back of fools and tells us not to cast pearls before swine. But sometimes, the swine do have to be dealt with. Parents bringing up children properly appeal *ad baculum* all the time. So do faithful leaders of state. So do cops with guns ("Drop it or I'll shoot!").

Not *ad baculum:* "If you do not see the wisdom of our laws against murder, perhaps you will be influenced by our death penalty."

Ad baculum: "If you don't vote for Senator Snuffles, then global warming will continue unabated, and we will all *die* from eating too much polar bear meat!"

The *ad hominem* fallacy occurs when the person is attacked instead of his argument. Again, this fallacy is not committed just because a man is attacked (form). Sometimes men need to be attacked, and it is not a fallacy to do so. Sometimes attacks focus the mind and—rather than being distracting—refocus the debate on the central issue. All these fallacies must have a latent value system built into them. The Second World War was not a massive example of the *ad hominem*.

Not *ad hominem:* "How can we believe you didn't steal this? You have lied to us so many times before."

Ad hominem: "Yes, we know that you maintain that triangles have three sides. But we also know that you're an evil man."

Bulverism occurs when an argument is *assumed* to be wrong, and then the one presenting the argument is attacked for *why* he believes it. This is a fallacy unless the person's reason for adopting the argument is truly relevant to your argument. The name Bulverism comes from an essay by C. S. Lewis in *God in the Dock,* in which he affectionately names this fallacy after an imaginary Ezekiel Bulver. This fallacious technique is frequently a distraction because the cause of one's arrival at a position can obviously be unrelated to its truth or falsity.

Not *Bulverism:* "You are running for Congress as an Independent today, but, just yesterday, you lost the Republican primary. You are just doing this because of personal ambition."

Bulverism: "You are saying that infants shouldn't be baptized because you grew up in a Baptist home."

The *tu quoque* fallacy means, in essence, "Yeah? Well, you do it too!" The fallacy is not happening when whatever it is you are doing is perfectly fine. A man guilty of this is therefore pointing out an inconsistency in his opponent's behavior and not defending inconsistency in his own behavior (which is what he needs to do).

Not *tu quoque:* "But you drink wine too."

Tu quoque: "But you smuggle cocaine too!"

The *ad ignorantiam* fallacy appeals to lack of information. It is, in effect, an argument from silence.

Not *ad ignorantiam:* "Why is there no mention of infant baptisms anywhere in the New Testament?"

Ad ignoratium: "There is no good reason published anywhere that shows how buckling up prevents aliens from sucking you out of your car. Better safe than sorry."

For it is a dog's eloquence, as Appius says, to undertake the task of abusing one's opponent.
—**Quintilian,** *Institutio Oratoria, vol. 4*

Chronological snobbery is when a position is rejected simply because of how old or new it is. Traditionalists commit this fallacy one way and modernists in another.

Not *chronological snobbery:* "I think that we should be more careful before we dismiss something our ancestors have done for centuries."

Chronological snobbery: "Modus ponens? That is so eighties!"

SUGGESTED READING

1. Aristotle, *Rhetoric*, II.IV.13—VI.8
2. Quintilian, *Institutio Oratoria*, vol. 2, VI.I.27—III.44
3. Optional: James B. Nance and Douglas J. Wilson, *Introductory Logic for Christian & Home Schools* (Moscow: Canon Press, 2006), ix–xiv, 217–243.

EXERCISE

1. Compose your own examples of each of these "fallacies" that would actually be legitimate to use in debate. Follow the form, but remove the fallacious distraction.

REVIEW QUESTIONS

1. What are fallacies of distraction?
2. What are fallacies of ambiguity?
3. What are fallacies of form?
4. What is the *ipse dixit* fallacy?
5. What is the *ad populum* fallacy?
6. What is an *ad baculum* fallacy?
7. What is an *ad hominem* fallacy?
8. What is a Bulverism?
9. What is a *tu quoque* fallacy?
10. What is an *ad ignoratiam* fallacy?
11. What is chronological snobbery?

Fallacies on the Street 2

We continue our foray into logic at work in the highways and byways of life. And in this chapter our concern is with fallacies of ambiguity.

With fallacies of distraction, the information that is offered in the argument is irrelevant to the conclusion presented. No, Abraham Lincoln was not the sixteenth president because we find it "convenient" to believe that. However, with fallacies of ambiguity the information is not so much irrelevant as it is fuzzy or confusing. There are various ways to do this. We've dealt with distraction, now onward into the world of shady (tough to pin) deceptions.

The *fallacy of equivocation* occurs when one of the terms in the argument has more than one meaning. This can happen because ordinary English words commonly have more than one meaning. If meanings are interchanged, but there is a pretense that this has not been done, then the fallacy of equivocation is there with all cylinders running. "Scripture says that God loves all men. Women aren't men. Therefore, we cannot say that God loves women." The ambiguity here concerns the generic use of *men* in the first premise (mankind), and the specific biological use of *men* (males) in the second premise. The meanings were changed mid-argument. That is equivocation.

The *fallacy of accent* occurs when a sentence can have its meaning changed completely by simply "italicizing" different words in the sentence. This is really a variant of equivocation. We can change the definitions of words by how we say them.

Take a statement like this: "I did not read the assigned book." A statement is made, and then, if it is challenged, the italics appear and move around to other points in the same sentence (which makes it

The same remark will seem freedom of speech in one's mouth, madness in another's, and arrogance in a third.
—**Quintilian,** *Institutio Oratoria, vol. 4*

look like nothing has changed), but in fact, everything in the argument has changed.

I did not read the assigned book—somebody else did.

I did *not* read the assigned book—emphatic denial.

I did not *read* the assigned book—I downloaded the audio version to my iPod.

I did not read the *assigned* book—I read another one by mistake. Maybe another edition.

I did not read the assigned *book*—It was a collection of articles. Again, the audio.

And so on.

Then there is the *fallacy of selective arrangement.* Suppose the parents of one of our students called and asked how the rhetoric course was going along, and he cheerfully reports to them that he is doing very well. When pressed for reasons for his cheerfulness, he says, "Well, for starters, I haven't seen Mr. Wilson with a joint this week." This is quite true, but the statement is made in such a way as to invite a conclusion that be slightly less than accurate.

The *fallacy of amphiboly* is where a sentence, taken as a whole, is ambiguous. Be alert. The world needs more lerts.

The *fallacy of composition* happens when someone thinks that whatever is true of the parts must be true of the whole. Every piece of a tank is lightweight. Therefore the tank is lightweight. This can be deceptive because sometimes it is quite true. Every piece of this tank is made out of metal. Therefore this tank is made out of metal.

Now the *fallacy of division.* This is the opposite of the fallacy of composition. This fallacy thinks that anything that is true of the whole must be true of the parts. For example, my car runs great on the open road. Therefore, if I take the bumper off, the bumper should run great on the open road. This example (like many logic examples) shows how ludicrous the fallacy can be when certain terms are employed. But it can be quite deceptive. Harvard is a bastion of intellectual prowess. He went to Harvard. Therefore, he must be an intellectual of the first rank.

In conclusion, a general point should be made here. This kind of fallacy happens all the time in doctrinal discussions. What you want to

Again, it is a fault to disparage an art or science or any occupation because of the faults of those engaged in it, as in the case of those who blame rhetoric because of the blameworthy life of some orator.

—*Rhetorica Ad Herennium*

do is keep track of all the players—what is every term in the argument, and what happens to it throughout the course of the argument?

SUGGESTED READING

1. Aristotle, *Rhetoric*, II.VI.9—VIII.12
2. Quintilian, *Institutio Oratoria*, vol. 2, VI.III.45—V.II

EXERCISE

1. Compose 300–500 words of sheer lighthearted argumentative brilliance. Do not commit any fallacies (not even once). Deliver publicly.

REVIEW QUESTIONS

1. What is a fallacy of equivocation?
2. What is a fallacy of accent?
3. What is a fallacy of selective arrangement?
4. What is the fallacy of amphiboly?
5. What is fallacy of composition?
6. What is the fallacy of division?

Fallacies on the Street 3

W e have considered fallacies of distraction as well as fallacies of ambiguity. We now come to fallacies of form. Please keep in mind that these are fallacies of form in informal logic. This means that an *informal* argument can have a structural problem just like a formal argument can have a structural problem.

Fallacies of distraction—look away!
Fallacies of ambiguity—what? huh?
Fallacies of form—structurally wobbly

The first problem is that of assuming what needs to be proven. This is called *petitio principii,* or begging the question. Another name for it is circular reasoning. A lot hinges on what we mean when we say "what needs to be proven." When someone challenges the honesty of honest Harry down at Honest Harry's Used Car Dealership, pointing at the sign does not greatly further the argument. His honesty is in question, and so consequently it does no good to rely on his honesty to settle the question.

At the same time, this fallacy can only be applied to what we might call creaturely questions. It does not and cannot apply to ultimate questions. We know there is a God because He has revealed Himself. How else could we know Him? Circular reasoning also helps us identify idols, like reason. Every finite creature must begin his reasoning axiomatically; he must begin somewhere. Everyone reasons in a circle when it comes to ultimate questions. And, when you're pushing someone in debate and they begin spinning in tight circles, you have found their god. It may be logic, personal preference, or popular opinion, but it is their idol. Make sure your own circularity is limited to places where you are comfortable worshipping.

Another problem is called *post hoc ergo propter hoc*, or (by its close friends) the *post hoc*. Translated, it means "after this therefore because of this." Another name for it is false cause. The argument takes this form: A occurred before B did. Therefore A is the cause of B. The fallacy occurs when the chronological priority is the only real reason given for the assumed causal relationship. After all, every true cause also precedes its effect in time. Or does it? Ponder your theology of time and the Creator.

But, to the extent we can grasp causal relations at all, we can say that reasons other than chronological priority should be given. The cue ball hit the eight ball before the eight ball went into the corner pocket. This gives us something other than chronological priority, that is, physical contact. But if we were to say that the president changed his mind two days after my letter to the *Daily Yawn* was published, and we did this in order to draw egocentric inferences, we would be yelling up the wrong logical rain spout.

Then there is the *either/or fallacy*. Another name for this is bifurcation. This occurs when a false (truncated) dilemma is presented. "You didn't vote for George W.? You must either be stupid or a communist." Obviously there might be many other reasons, and the questioner has limited them in a way advantageous to himself (which can also be a form of "straw man" reasoning, where a speaker sets up his opposition in an unfair way, so that it is easy to take down). But the fallacy is not operative just because only two options are presented. To say that a sports car can only be black or white is not the same thing as saying that a choice to commit adultery is black and white. Sometimes there really are just two options. Consider this: the sun is shining or it is not shining. If we exclude equivocation, and thoroughly define our terms, then we really do have just two possibilities.

Now we come to the *complex question*, sometimes known as the loaded question. In this problem, the question is framed in such a way as to exclude a legitimate response. To use an easy example: "Have you attended all your classes sober this week?" *Yes* accepts the implication that last week you didn't, and *no* means you are a lush now. The only legitimate way out for the respondent is to say something like, "Wait a minute . . ." A good indicator that someone is cheating in an argument this way is

We shall make our adversaries unpopular by setting forth their violent behavior, their dominance, factiousness, wealth, lack of self-restraint, high birth, clients, hospitality, club allegiance, or marriage alliances, and by making clear that they rely more upon these supports than upon the truth. We shall bring our adversaries into contempt by presenting their idleness, cowardice, sloth, and luxurious habits.
—*Rhetorica Ad Herennium*

when they press the point, refusing to hear any qualifications whatso-ever. "Don't waffle on me. Just say yes or no." When this happens, just say complex question. This is a good time and place to bring in the name of the fallacy, which is not always the case. Even better though (if you have the rhetorical chops and aren't nervous and shrill) is to spring the trap of the loaded question with half a gallon of unthreatened 80 proof sarcasm. "I'm drunk on you, babe. Your aura is overpowering." *haha*

And lastly, we must deal with *apriorism,* or hasty generalization. This occurs when someone engages in high-speed (or eccentric) induction. There are nevertheless intangibles here—this is an informal fallacy of form, which has a correct form technically. "Herbert is a misogynist. I hate men."

SUGGESTED READING

1. Aristotle, *Rhetoric,* II.VIII.13—X.II
2. Quintilian, *Institutio Oratoria,* vol. 3, VII.Preface.I—II.34

EXERCISE

1. Compose a 500 word argument for something that you believe to be true, and attempt to commit all five of the fallacies mentioned here (humor is fine). Is it easy or hard to slip into that type of reasoning? Note that having the truth is no antidote to muddle-headed reasoning. Present publicly.

REVIEW QUESTIONS

1. What is *petitio principii?*
2. What is a *post hoc ergo propter hoc?*
3. What is the either/or fallacy?
4. What is a complex question?
5. What is apriorism?

LESSON 17

The Poetry of Argument

Let art, then, imitate nature.
—*Rhetorica Ad Herennium*

Understanding the fundamentals of logic in argument is important, but it is not the only important thing. We have already talked about the importance of ethos and pathos, and our topic here is related to this, but not identical to it. Poetic expression is the potent matter of both ethos and style; it is where your closed fist meets an unsuspecting face. Sound logos is the straight wrist, the rotating shoulders and hips, the assurance that, once your fist connects, the opponent will immediately discover a certain wobbliness in the knees.

C.S. Lewis once pointed out there are three basic ways of using language. Two of them are divergent ways of communicating more accurately what we mean.

Ordinary: "It is very cold outside."

Scientific: "It is currently 17 degrees below zero at the airport."

Poetic: "Ah, bitter chill it was! The owl, for all his feathers, was a-cold; The hare limped trembling through the frozen grass, And silent was the flock in woolly fold: Numb were the Beadman's fingers" (Keats, "The Eve of St. Agnes," stanza I).

Now a certain mentality exists that says only the second way of speaking can be properly called more "accurate." This mentality relates to modernity like ugly to an ape, or perhaps like white to rice. It assumes that every intellectual problem has a solution when the following criteria, which are necessary to the method, are employed in finding that solution. The method requires *precision*; it requires *quantification*; it requires *abstraction*; and the method requires *direct correlation*. This is the analytic paradigm.

In contrast, we have the poetic paradigm. The approach of poetry—which includes metaphor, simile, personification, etc.—requires *imprecision*; it requires *qualification*; it uses *concrete images*; and the approach requires *oblique correlation.* And, ironically, it also helps communicate more accurately. That's right. You heard us.

When a woman is in labor, a nurse will frequently ask her to rate her pain on a scale of 1 to 10. Moderns love to quantify. But what does that scale even mean? Is 1 equal to a childhood pillow fight and 10 equal to the Battle of the Bulge? Or is it arbitrary and metric—Painometers, 10 of which equal 1 Painogram?

Poets love to qualify and compare. The pain is like this, but not like that. It's not as bad as before, but there's more pressure. Seventeen degrees below zero at the airport? (Do you even know what a degree is, or how you count them, or where they all hide when there are zero of them at the airport?) It's so cold your nostrils will freeze shut but not your eyelids. Qualification successfully communicates vicarious experience. Quantification rarely does (without a great deal of help from the listener).

The language of religion, the language of ultimate things, requires the poetic approach, and this affects more than just the conclusion of our arguments. It must affect how we argue. "God is an immutable Spirit who only works perfection." This is quite true but tells us less than, "God is a Rock, and His work is perfect." Here we learn more from a statement that is, strictly speaking, not true. God is not a Rock, and rocks don't work, much less work perfectly. And yet, from something less true, we can learn more truth. This is because of how God made the world.

This is not a battle between "logic" or "math" on the one hand and the "humanities" on the other. Math and science rightly understood are liberal arts. We must recognize that these various disciplines are different precisely because the "rules" which guide them vary.

Properly understood, these disciplinary constraints are not so different that they exclude the disciplines from being gathered together under the Seven Liberal Arts. Never forget that the Quadrivium included arithmetic, astronomy, and geometry. The fourth part of it, music, has an important aspect which the nonmathematical can never enjoy. Grammar, dialectic and rhetoric are more obviously in the realm of the humanities, but they are also preliminary studies.

Now if to discern what is written artistically proves your mastery of the art, then a far better proof of this mastery is to write artistically yourself.
—*Rhetorica Ad Herennium*

So if this is the case, then why all the hubbub? In one realm, everything is predictable, regular, defined strictly, abstract, logically arranged, and not really a matter of private opinion. But in another realm, the varied elements are concrete, irregular, not demonstrable, grouped in countless debatable ways. Accuracy is important here, but it is evaluated by different criteria, and is therefore not tested as easily. Neither approach has a problem, but we must answer the question whether we should allow the attributes of either to dictate to the other. When this happens, we have forgotten the importance of sphere sovereignty.

Properly understood, mathematical thinking provides outstanding training in understanding the nature of limits or boundaries. But this should include the nature of the limits of math. The drive behind mathematical rationalism is really the desire for certainty. We want epistemic certainty—but we can never have the same certainty from induction as we do from deduction, and we can never know if we have handled a poem as well as a multiplication table. I could select some mathematical problem and know my handling of it to be inerrant. I could never say that about an interpretation of a poem, any poem, including one of my own.

The poetic nature of this has to be understood as part of the argumentation. Another way of saying this is that logos cannot be completely separated from ethos and pathos. And this leads to a series of questions and considerations:

When the Good Samaritan discovered the fellow who had been beaten, did he find him on the right side of the road or the left? Prove it. We can't listen to a story like this without picturing it, and we can't picture it without the "camera angle."

Picture Frodo and Sam being chased down a hillside by a pack of about fifteen ravening orcs. Now, are they running to the right, to the left, down the hill toward you, or down the hill away from you? This is the same point about camera angle.

Four apples added to three apples will give you seven in all. How does this make you feel? One plus one equals two, right? Well, not if they're rabbits.

The Lord is good; His mercies are constant and unfailing. When I had fallen, He picked me up; when I had slipped His hand sustained me.

Others are the victims of a more arrogant form of sloth; they assume a stern air and let their beards grow, and, as though despising the precepts of oratory, sit for a while in the schools of the philosophers, that, by an assumption of a severe mien before the public gaze and by an affected contempt of others they may assert their moral superiority, while leading a life of debauchery at home. For philosophy may be counterfeited, but eloquence never.
—**Quintilian,** *Institutio Oratoria, vol. 4*

The Lord God of hosts is without change in all He does. His goodness endures forever. Outline this. Now if we were trained to outline in the Western way, we would begin with a Roman numeral I, and move on from there. But the outline here should show that it is a chiasm (A, B, C, C', B', A').

When men engage in abstractions, they are basically doing one of two things. If their approach is Hellenistic, they in some fashion think of form and matter as distinct entities which can be separated. They are defining. They do this, either by extracting form from matter, or subtracting matter from the standing essential form. The Hellenistic way of knowing is therefore via some kind of subtraction. If they are Hebraic in their (and I hesitate to use the word) "abstractions," they are describing. The Hebraic epistemology (and may I add, the poetic epistemology) recognizes the concrete and particular. The Hebraic way of knowing is therefore via addition.

Adam was told to name the animals, not to define them. Naming considers attributes and includes the observed characteristics in the name. This is very different from extracting the attributes. A bird should be named while it is still flying. As Rushdoony puts it, "Abstract knowledge is the attempt to interpret all things without reference to God. God is abstracted from reality, and things are interpreted, not in terms of God, but in terms of themselves."[1]

> But to avoid all display of art in itself requires consummate art.
> —**Quintilian,** *Institutio Oratoria, vol. 2*

SUGGESTED READING

1. Aristotle, *Rhetoric,* II.XI.I—XVI.4
2. Quintilian, *Institutio Oratoria,* vol. 3, VII.II.35—VIII.7

1. R. J. Rushdoony, *Revolt Against Maturity: A Biblical Psychology of Man* (Fairfax: Thoburn Press, 1977), 23.

EXERCISE

1. Compose two short creative (descriptive) sketches. First, a 250 word *analytic* description of a spring day. Limit yourself to *precision, quantification, abstraction,* and *direct correlation.* Second, write a 250 word poetic description of a math problem. Limit yourself to *imprecision, qualification, concrete images,* and *oblique correlation.* Present both publicly.

REVIEW QUESTIONS

1. What is the difference between expressions that are ordinary, scientific, and poetic?
2. Name three elements in the poetic approach to meaning.
3. What is the difference between how we handle a poem and how we handle a mathematical table?
4. In the parable of the Good Samaritan, was the fellow who was beat up on the right side of the road or the left? Discuss.
5. What is a chiasm?
6. How might this affect an outline?

LESSON 18

INVENTION, STASIS, AND THE

Exordium

In giving a prepared talk or lecture, as a general rule, the preparation of your *exordium* should come last. An individual usually (unless especially gifted in the psychic arts) cannot introduce someone if he doesn't know his name. In the same way, a speaker cannot introduce his talk, preparing his listeners to hear it in all wisdom, unless he knows *what* he is talking about. And he can't know that until his talk is in some fashion *there* to be introduced.

An old adage about public speaking is that you should tell them what you are going to tell them, then tell them, and then tell them what you told them. While it is not quite so simple, there is a great deal of basic structural wisdom there.

While the talk does not have to be finished and polished before you prepare the exordium, at a minimum you need to have a good grasp of the outline. This relates to *stasis theory*, which is a matter of learning how to ask and answer the right questions. This in turn helps in preparing the outline of the address, which then sets the stage for the exordium.

This whole issue of stasis is one of those obvious things that has probably always been around, but scholars credit Hermagoras with the codification of it. We do not have his text, but his basic approach has been reconstructed from discussions of it in Cicero, Quintilian, et al.

The word *stasis* comes from the Greek word meaning a "stand." A speaker uses stasis theory in picking his ground, where he will stand, what hill he will die on, etc. In a debate situation, the stand refers to the point of collision, the point of disagreement, the hinge upon which all turns. Put another way, what is the issue? What is the *point?* In many rhetorical settings, this question could be asked with great profit.

The sole purpose of the exordium is to prepare our audience in such a way that they will be disposed to lend a ready ear to the rest of our speech.
—**Quintilian,** *Institutio Oratoria, vol. 2*

The old rule still holds good that no unusual word, no overbold metaphor, no phrase derived from the lumber-rooms of antiquity or from poetic licence should be detected in the *exordium.*
—**Quintilian,** *Institutio Oratoria, vol. 2*

If the hearers have been fatigued by listening, we shall open with something that may provoke laughter—a fable, a plausible fiction, a caricature, an ironical inversion of the meaning of a word, an ambiguity, innuendo, banter, a naivety, an exaggeration, a recapitulation, a pun, an unexpected turn, a comparison, a novel tale, a historical anecdote, a verse, or a challenge or a smile of approbation directed at some one.
—*Rhetorica Ad Herennium*

The audience looks to the speaker for guidance here. If the speaker knows what is going on, the audience will continue to look to the speaker as a guide. If the speaker is confident (as opposed to being simply a blustering fool), they will look to him for direction.

Now issues can be divided into two kinds: *specific* and *general*, or to use another set of names, *definite* and *indefinite.*

Specific or definite: the issue here (*hypothesis*) involves actual situations, persons, places, events. A classic example of this would be: should Cato marry?

General or indefinite: the issue here (*thesis*) involves situations that have a broad area of application, which do not refer to actual situations on the ground. A classic example of this is: should a person marry?

These general questions can be divided further. Quintilian called them "questions of knowledge" on the one hand and "questions of actions" on the other. A question of knowledge asks, for example, what is the proper relationship between church and state. A question of action asks whether a particular minister should run for Congress. In this, it should be obvious that the latter kind of question cannot be answered without appealing to the answer you derived from the first kind of question. The same thing is also true with our earlier division.

This brings us to the four *staseis.* Hermagoras (from what we can gather) formulated four basic questions, or staseis.

1. *Conjecture:* Is there something to talk about? Does it exist? Did it happen?
2. *Definition:* And what kind of thing or event is it anyway?
3. *Quality:* Do we approve or disapprove? Was it right or wrong?
4. *Procedure:* What is the course of action? What should we do?

Weapons are superfluous for one who does not know what his target is.
—**Quintilian**, *Institutio Oratoria, vol. 2*

The best way to illustrate these "hinges" would be by pointing to how a defense attorney might want to defend his client against a charge of murder. "First, it was not murder at all. The deceased simply had a heart attack." This is conjecture. "Yes, my client killed him, but it was entirely accidental. The charge should be manslaughter, not murder at all." This is definition. "Yes, my client killed him, and it was high time somebody did. My client has always been public-spirited that way." This is quality. "Yes, my client killed him, but, as much as we disapprove, we have to recognize that my client is not in his right mind." This is procedure. And of course, he needs to be careful how he slides from one to the other. If you take your stand somewhere, you need to *stand* there. You should not say, "My client did not do it, was not there at the time, and besides, if he did do it, it was an accident, and he's crazy anyway."

> In general, it is better to pass by not only that which weakens the cause but also that which neither weakens nor helps it.
> —*Rhetorica Ad Herennium*

SUGGESTED READING

1. Aristotle, *Rhetoric*, II.XVII.I—XX.5
2. *Rhetorica Ad Herennium*, II.I.I—II.VI.9
3. Quintilian, *Institutio Oratoria*, vol. 3, VII.IX.I—VIII.III.19

EXERCISE

1. Where you choose to stand comes down to the relationship you have to your audience and their degree of hostility and disagreement. Take a single thesis (or hypothesis) and write four different short arguments (250 words), each one emphasizing disagreement at a different stasis. Focus on using the poetic paradigm in all of them. Present your strongest one publicly.

> The style of the exordium should not resemble that of our purple patches . . . it should rather seem simple and unpremeditated, while neither our words nor our looks should promise too much.
> —**Quintilian,** *Institutio Oratoria, vol. 2*

REVIEW QUESTIONS

1. What is stasis theory?
2. Where does the word *stasis* come from?
3. What is the difference between a definite (or specific) and indefinite (or general) issue?
4. What is hypothesis?
5. What is the thesis?
6. Give an example of each.
7. What does Quintilian say about subdividing the general questions further?

8. What are the four staseis?

9. What is the rhetor doing in the first stasis?

10. The second?

11. The third?

12. Fourth?

13. Can a stasis ever be left out?

INVENTION, STASIS, AND THE

Narratio

The *narratio* is where the speaker lays out the lumber he will use to build his magnificent structure, when he eventually gets to it. Consequently, he wants to make sure he has everything he needs and very little which he does not need. As with assembling a trike on Christmas Eve, you should be worried if you have a lot of parts left over.

As we turn our attention to invention and the narratio, let us review the four staseis. In the first stasis, the rhetor wondereth if he and the audience agree over the *existence* of some entity or the commission of some act. In the second stasis, the rhetor determines if he and the audience concur on the *classification* of that thing or act. In the third, he tries to determine if he and the audience agree on the *quality* of the act or perhaps the seriousness of it. And in the fourth, he urges a course of action based upon his success in bringing his audience with him thus far.

Now suppose the speaker has a hostile audience. If this is the case, then he will have to fight for every inch, going through all four staseis. It is even possible, where there is dispute and significant disagreement, that he will not make it past the first stasis. But if a man has a friendly audience, the rub may be at one simple point in one of the later staseis, and if he establishes his point there, everything else is smooth sledding.

In identifying the basic point at issue, we are looking for honesty, not neutrality. Remember that there is no such thing as neutrality. The narratio is not a "neutral" statement of the facts, after which the speaker goes on to reveal his "biased" opinion. The narratio is *part* of the argument. Put another way, your argument does not begin with the confirmatio. But discretion is still important. Subtlety, which is not to be confused with dishonesty, is an important part of argumentation.

I hold that the statement of fact more than any portion of the speech should be adorned with the utmost grace and charm.
—**Quintilian,** *Institutio Oratoria, vol. 2*

A hostile audience should not have any factual quibbles with what is presented in the narratio. Their squealing should come later, over the interpretation and usage of those facts.

The speaker should (of course) have established his ethos early on in the narratio. He should also have established key assumptions or definitions in the course of his narratio. He who defines, wins. He should not introduce any new premises after the narratio. "Oh, yeah. Here is something else I need to make this argument work. I forgot." In the building of the narratio, he should have quietly closed off at least some of his adversary's routes of escape.

In establishing the stasis, a speaker is asking himself certain questions about the talk as a whole. He then knows what to gather when he puts together his narratio. Here are some of the first questions he needs to ask. And he should deal with the first two questions before going through conjecture, definition, etc.

1. He should decide whether or not he wants to make his case as a thesis or hypothesis.

2. If he goes with thesis, he should decide whether or not he wants the talk to be theoretical or practical.

3. Having got thus far, he should decide which of the four staseis most deal with the essential point before the house. In other words, where should he start his discussion? Just because the first stasis is conjecture does not mean that the talk should begin there. It might go without saying. But of course, it also might not.

According to Cicero, the work of conjecture can be done by asking four different kinds of question.

1. Does it exist? Is it true?
2. Where did it start?
3. What is the cause?
4. Can it be altered or changed?

When he gets to definition, these are the kinds of question to ask.

1. What kind of thing is it?
2. What larger category contains this thing?
3. What are its parts, and what are their relations?

Questions about quality can be done two ways. Questions can be simple, or they can be comparative:

Simple:
1. Is this good or bad?
2. Should it be avoided or sought out?
Comparative:
This can be complicated and/or dicey.
1. Is this better or worse than the alternative?
2. Is it more desirable than the available alternatives? Less desirable?

When the questions about procedure arise, it is important to note that procedural questions will not come up directly in the narratio. But questions of procedure need to have been addressed in the speaker's mind—he needs to know how the narratio will be applied. The speaker should know what he is going to suggest later and have it play a role in composing his narratio.

So, let us turn our attention *ad scenariones.* How would these questions relate to an assigned speech about say, evolution?

Conjecture: Is the theory of evolution true? Did it actually happen? If the audience he is addressing is a national convention of secular geologists, the speaker should plan on spending *all* his time here. Questions of conjecture have identified the point at issue.

Definition: Suppose this is a convention of open-minded secular geologists, which is a big suppose, but suppose this is the case. The speaker may get a chance to speak about microevolution, variation within species, which no creationist denies. Under the heading of conjecture, he has rejected macroevolution, but he has created the need for further definition.

A Statement of Facts should have three qualities: brevity, clarity, and plausibility.
—*Rhetorica Ad Herennium*

Of course, if the theory of macroevolution is false, then it can hardly be good to praise these falsehoods. Questions of quality address whether or not we should condemn or praise what we have established in the first two questions.

And then, what should we do about it? The theory is false, so we should quit teaching it. The truth of microevolution is an observable phenomenon, so there is no problem with telling schoolchildren we have observed it.

SUGGESTED READING

1. Aristotle, *Rhetoric*, II.XX.6—XXII.8.
2. *Rhetorica Ad Herennium*, II.VI.10—XIII.20
3. Quintilian, *Institutio Oratoria*, vol. 3, VIII.III.20—V.35

EXERCISE

1. Pick a thesis statement and a hostile audience, then compose a 300 word narratio that would fit perfectly into a longer speech or paper. It should not read like a list of facts, nor should it contain explicit arguments. It should read like an interesting situational sketch, out of which, terrific arguments could be built. Present publicly.

REVIEW QUESTIONS

1. Is your narratio part of your argument?
2. Where do you establish your definitions?
3. What are some questions you might ask in conjecture?
4. Definition?
5. Quality?
6. Procedure?

LESSON 20

INVENTION, STASIS, AND THE

Confirmatio and Refutatio

The *confirmatio* is where the speaker assembles the pieces. The *refutatio* is where he tries to keep his worthy adversary from being able to disassemble the pieces.

First, the speaker should seek to recall what brought him around to this position. Presumably he is arguing a position which he actually holds. How did he come to hold this position? A good exercise would be to list the reasons. He can then throw away those which seemed compelling at the time but now, in the light of day, seem so much less so.

Also, a speaker needs to anticipate what his opponents will actually say in response to him. In the refutatio, there is a cheap and easy way to discover what your opponents might say, and that is to discover what they actually *do* say. In anticipating the refutatio, the temptation will be to go in one of two directions. The first is the obvious temptation to avoid research and come to your confirmatio all prepared to wing it. The second temptation is to be encyclopedic. This is where the speaker lists all his opponents' arguments and then works through them in some kind of alphabetic order. While some debate judges may want you to leave no stone unturned—gotta answer them *all*—there is a rhetorical problem here.

In forming and answering arguments, a speaker must understand the nature of a strategic point. A point is strategic when it meets two criteria: being both decisive and feasible. In military terms, a point is decisive when, if captured, the enemy's cause is lost. It is feasible if you can do it. In terms of cultural evangelism, a community is strategic if a great deal more is lost to the enemy when that point is lost. It is feasible when it is reasonable to suppose that it can actually be done. In advancing the dominion of Christ, why don't we all move to Bovill, Idaho? We

But we must be equally on our guard against the obscurity which results from excessive abridgment, and it is better to say a little more than is necessary than a little less.
—**Quintilian,** *Institutio Oratoria, vol. 2*

could take the town within a couple of minutes. It is feasible, but not decisive. Why don't we all move to New York City, and have at it there? Decisive, but not feasible.

So in a collision of arguments, do not waste time refuting twigs when you can take down the trunk. If the trunk goes, the twigs go, even if you have not mentioned them. At the same time, remember the importance of ethos (meaning, remember the importance of the audience). If your opponent got a laugh, let us say, with one of his twigs, then you need to deal with it. Otherwise people may go away remembering what he said, but not remembering how it was countered.

Remember also that if a speaker is good at getting at the trunk of an argument, the adversary will have no alternative but to attack his ethos in an *ad hominem* way. The speaker needs to take care not to help him. Become a pompous fancy pants, and personal attacks will stick on contact. It is easy to be too clever by half.

In considering the various possible points of stasis, it is crucial to grasp the idea of the inescapable concept. The inescapable concept works this way: not whether, but which. The issues involved here can include God and gods, law, faith, imposition of morality, etc. As the speaker, you need to ask questions concerning inescapable concepts at each stasis. Otherwise, you might breeze right by the strategic point. And when you have that point, steal some thunder.

Use stasis theory for more than discovering where you and your adversaries differ. You want to find the point where you differ on a *sine qua non* of his position, and you want to find a *sine qua non* of his position which can be "captured." *Sine qua non* means "without which not." A *sine qua non* of the opposing position means that without that argument, that position is lost.

> *Conjecture:* Does it exist?
> *Definition:* If it does, what kind of "it" is it?
> *Quality:* What do we think about it?
> *Procedure:* What do we do about it?

Now though laughter may be regarded as a trivial matter, and an emotion frequently awakened by buffoons, actors or fools, it has a certain imperious force of its own which it is very hard to resist.
—**Quintilian,** *Institutio Oratoria, vol. 2*

Wit always appears to greater advantage in reply than in attack.
—**Quintilian,** *Institutio Oratoria, vol. 2*

SUGGESTED READING

1. Aristotle, *Rhetoric*, II.XXII.9—XXIII.II
2. *Rhetorica Ad Herennium*, II.XIV.2I—XXI.34
3. Quintilian, *Institutio Oratoria*, vol. 3, VIII.VI.I—IX.I.45

EXERCISE

1. Compose a 500 word confirmatio, assembling your arguments from the material laid out in your previously written narratio. Stay focused on your originally conceived thesis statement. Once this is written, predict your hostile audience's reaction. Compose a 500 word refutatio, anticipating, deflecting, and deflating their inevitable attacks on your confirmatio. Deliver the pair publicly.

REVIEW QUESTIONS

1. What is the simplest way to proceed in your invention for your refutatio?
2. What is a strategic point?
3. What is an inescapable concept?
4. How does this knowledge help you in preparing a talk?

LESSON 21

Invention and Arrangement

As mentioned earlier, according to the ancients, arrangement was second in importance only to invention. How a man assembles his lecture, oration, talk, sharing, or whatever is very important. "What I want to do is this." There are two parts to the process. In the invention, he has come up with a pile of arguments, a number of things to say. The first step in arrangement is picking which of these arguments will be used, and the second is placing them in an order that is clear and persuasive.

If the audience is completely ignorant of the subject, then the speaker does not need to spend any significant time on a refutatio. There is no need to administer poisons in order to demonstrate consummate skill with antidotes. If they are hostile toward the position, the speaker needs to spend extra time defusing that hostility.

Take care not to put too many eggs in the pudding. Just because it was taught in "ancient rhetoric" does not mean that we gotta do it. Both Aristotle and Plato complained about the overly subtle distinctions made by some rhetors in the study of arrangement, and their complaint had substance. But there is a natural structure to ancient oratory that is quite helpful. You've already worked on three major components in the last two exercises. You have the head and torso; now it's time to give your mannequin legs and make it walk around.

This is the general pattern:

I. Exordium—Quintilian said the sole point of the exordium is to prepare the audience to listen to the rest. It comes from the Latin meaning "to urge forward." Cicero recommended two kinds of exordia, which were the introduction and the insinuation. There were also five kinds of situations a speaker might face. The case might be honorable, in which

> But these rules of style, while part of the student's theoretical knowledge, are not in themselves sufficient to give him oratorical power.
> —**Quintilian**, *Institutio Oratorio, vol. 4*

case no exordium was needed. In a difficult case, use insinuation. With mean, ambiguous, or obscure cases, use an introduction, which goes straight up the middle. Insinuations are the more difficult to write and should be almost exclusively used when dealing with hostile (as opposed to merely ignorant) audiences.

Remember the point of exordia. The speaker wants to make the audience attentive in the first place and receptive in the second. Make them attentive: show the importance of the issue; show its importance to them; show the importance of the subject to the universe generally. Make them care. Make them want more. Make them receptive: strengthen ethos; weaken the ethos of those so hardy as to oppose the truth; respect your audience; praise your position (with discretion). But don't go too far. This is a hook, a taste, an open door, and an invitation.

2. NARRATIO—Cicero thought the narratio could be dispensed with if the audience was up to speed. However, Quintilian was not at all of this mind. The kind of case being dealt with affects how the facts are arranged and stated in the narratio. Quintilian also said that we should state the facts in a manner consistent with the facts which we want believed. In defending someone accused of theft, a speaker wants to show they do not have a covetous bone in their body. If accusing them, the speaker himself has seen them fondling merchandise in all the stores around town.

But remember, the narratio is not yet argument. The speaker is, however, presenting facts from which the argument will be drawn, and these should be consistent with that argumentation. So with the arrangement, prepare the narratio depending on the kind of audience anticipated. If they are hostile, reserve scandalous facts about the accused, for example, until after *your* ethos is up and running. It is difficult to write a complete narratio without slipping into dry statistical prose. Turn your style up; make it interesting even if your audience is only watching you set the stage. It is also difficult to keep yourself from building arguments and drawing conclusions. In the post-blog era, we are prone to write as we think and think in anti-linear MTV spasms. Discipline yourself. Hold back your punches (for the time being).

In a word, the function of eloquence in teaching is not to make people like what was once offensive, or to make them do what they were loth to do, but to make clear what was hidden from them.
—**Saint Augustine**, *On Christian Teaching*

3. PARTITIO—In a longer partitio, the speaker makes clear to the audience which issues must be addressed by any participant in the discussion. And second, he also outlines for them the order in which his proofs will appear. This orients them and makes them happy, which is good. Quintilian uses the illustration of how mile markers make a journey go more swiftly. The speaker is serving the auditors and must not be patronizing. In a shorter partitio, the speaker simply sticks pins in the battlefield map of the narratio. Opponents are . . . here . . . here . . . and here. The final pin (your own position) comes next.

4. PROPOSITIO—This is your thesis statement (or hypothesis). It can be at the end of the partito or stuck somewhere in the middle. It can even bat lead-off. Stick it wherever you think it will be most effective. The speaker does not really need to know how to arrange his propositio as a whole, but he should spend a good bit of time arranging the words of that sentence or sentences. The propositio ought to be directly related to what falls out of your stasis analysis. What is the point of the talk?

5. CONFIRMATIO AND REFUTATIO—Quintilian thought (and so should you) that strong arguments should each stand alone and should each be treated at length. Weaker arguments (if you must use them at all) should be clustered together so that they might lean on one another for support. He said that they may not have the force of a thunderbolt, but they might manage to have the collective destructive force of hail. The speaker should not trot out his weakest argument first. And Quintilian, for his part, says he should not place them last. This means, for those who have been following, that they should come in the middle. They may support one another, and stronger, more independent arguments hold them up on either side, like bookends. Do not confuse these two parts of the speech. The confirmatio supports your propositio. It builds a castle around it. The refutatio (aware that Vikings are only attracted to castles) defends the walls, anticipates the points of assault, and *cuts them off.* It is helpful to think of the goal of the refutatio as preservation of the confirmatio. If you've done your job, a preserved confirmatio means an established propositio.

6. PERORATIO—According to Cicero, a speaker should accomplish three things in his conclusion. First he sums up what he has argued (logos). Secondly, he should put a dent in the ethos of those who oppose the case (ethos, kind of). And third, he should arouse sympathy for the case (pathos). Modern writing, however, can be very clunky in this respect. Be wary of simple summary. Be confident (but don't gloat). Allude to what has been proven and defeated by standing by a road pointing in the direction that is now inevitable, given what you've established.

SUGGESTED READING

> 1. Aristotle, *Rhetoric*, II.XXIII.12—XXIII.30
> 2. *Rhetorica Ad Herennium*, II.XXII.34—II.XXXI.50
> 3. Quintilian, *Institutio Oratoria*, vol. 3, IX.II.1—III.15

EXERCISE

There can be no doubt that the best method of correction is to put aside what we have written for a certain time, so that when we return to it after an interval it will have the air of novelty and of being another's handiwork.
—**Quintilian,** *Institutio Oratorio, vol. 4*

> 1. Write a short partitio/propositio (150 words) to fit between your already composed narratio and confirmatio/refutatio. Write a peroratio (200–250 words). Now that you know your speech, write the exordium (200–250 words). Put it all together and edit and overhaul like the dickens. Remove all your nonsense and redundancies. Think of your audience and adhere to the golden rule—don't give them anything you wouldn't enjoy hearing yourself. Present the whole resurrected and improved thing publicly.

REVIEW QUESTIONS

> 1. What did Quintilian say the exordium is for?
> 2. What should you guard against in the narratio?
> 3. What illustration did Quintilian use to describe the partitio?
> 4. What should you do with a collection of weaker arguments?
> 5. What should be avoided in the conclusion?

6. What are the two steps in arrangement?

7. What are the two types of exordia?

8. According to Cicero, what are the five types of situation which you might face?

9. Give an example of each.

10. What did Quintilian say the narratio had to do?

11. What do you do in the partitio?

12. What should the arrangement of your arguments be in your confirmatio? Why?

13. What do you do in the peroratio?

The Rhythm of Words: I

As the reader can see from the title of the chapter, our topic concerns the rhythm of words, but the point is broader than words. Not only would I like you to consider what is written here, and learn to write a sonnet thereby, but also to note the structure of what is being said, that you might have some illustration, however clumsy, of what the heck you are supposed to be trying to learn in this book.

Until now, we have been considering the larger arrangement of a talk; the point of this section is to pay some attention to the arrangement of words in phrases and sentences—to consider the cadences of words. The best way to do this is to learn some of the fundamental considerations in poetry; these things can then be applied to prose oration. Most likely (unless you have some sort of latent gift or prior training), your compositions have not exactly been fine wine. And that's not a bad thing. But even if they were, improvement (especially stylistic improvement) is always possible.

With this in mind, our attention turns to the topic at hand. What is poetry? The question cannot be answered with great precision, at least not without self-contradiction. However, even though we may not be able to determine the exact boundaries of poetry, it is important that we establish a general notion of what we are talking about. One writer defines it as "a patterned form of verbal or written expression of ideas in concentrated, imaginative, and rhythmical terms." Burton Raffel defines poetry as a "disciplined, compact verbal utterance, in some more or less musical mode, dealing with aspects of internal or external reality in some meaningful way." John Ciardi says, "So for poetry. The concern is not to arrive at a definition and to close the book, but to arrive at an experience. There will never be a complete system for 'understanding'

definitions of poetry

experience + understanding

107

or for 'judging' poetry." Judson Jerome allows that there is something to the definition which simply says poetry is "metrical writing." Lewis Turco defines poetry as "the art of language." So what shall we make of all this? For my money, poetry is the metrical use of words and figures in imaginative and concentrated form.

> A poem is a thought that comes out sounding good
> And lingers a while, but it doesn't have to rhyme.
>   Though it could.

But our interest is not going to be defining poetry in general, but rather writing a particular kind of poem that you will have to read in public at some point. Perhaps the reader might want to have some knowledge of the constituent parts of an English sonnet, since that will be the exercise. And why will that be the exercise? Because writing formal poetry is good for the brain, good for the world (either as inspiration or compost), and is the rhetorical equivalent of doing lots of linguistic pushups. Writing poetry is the best of all prose exercises.

What is meter? In our language, syllables are either stressed or unstressed. A stressed syllable is also known as an accented syllable, or a long syllable. It is signified with an accent mark ('). An unstressed syllable is called the unaccented or short syllable. It is marked thus: (-). Take the word strawberry, for example. This is pronounced STRAWberry, and the accents for this word would look this way (' - -). In a line of poetry, given all the different possible combinations of words, the possible variations of meter are considerable. But in most poetry, part of the point is to make the meter somewhat predictable and readily identifiable. To make this easier, we have identified units of meter called feet.

So then, what is a foot? A metrical foot consists of two or three syllables. It is a "molecule" of meter. When we learn to identify these units of meter, we can more readily identify the metrical structure of a line of poetry. A foot usually consists of one stressed syllable and one or two unstressed syllables. Depending on the relationship of stressed to unstressed syllables, we have given these units different names. The basic feet are called iambic, trochaic, anapestic, and dactylic. You will be writing iambic poetry in our exercise, but you should have some acquaintance with the meters you are trying to avoid (or pursue on your own).

What is an iambic foot? An iambic foot (or an iamb) is a two-syllable word, or two syllables in a row, with the stress on the second syllable. The iamb is the most common foot in English poetry, and when you have a string of them, the result is almost immediately recognizable as metrical. An iamb looks like this (- '). Many two-syllable words are self-contained iambs, such as police, delight, or bemuse. Examples of two-syllable words that are not iambs would be bookcase or very. Ironically, iamb is not an iamb. Note the iambic feet in the following lines.

Eternity and time confound
The buckling minds of mortal men

What is a trochaic foot? A trochaic foot (or a trochee) is a two-syllable word, or two syllables in a row, in which the stress comes first (' -). Examples were given above (bookcase and very), and others are easy enough to find—ever, happy, and parrot. Mark the trochaic feet in these famous lines from Macbeth.

By the pricking of my thumbs
Something wicked this way comes

What is an anapestic foot? An anapestic foot (or an anapest) is a three-syllable word, or three syllables in a row, consisting of two unstressed syllables followed by a stressed syllable (- - '). Examples of anapestic words would be intertwine and cavalier. Mark the anapests in the two last lines from Byron's "The Destruction of Sennacherib."

And the might of the Gentile, unsmote by the sword,
Hath melted like snow in the glance of the Lord!

What is a dactylic foot? A dactylic foot (or a dactyl) is a three-syllable word, or three syllables in a row, consisting of a stressed syllable followed

The best judge as to rhythm is the ear, which appreciates fullness of rhythm or feels the lack of it, is offended by harshness, soothed by smooth and excited by impetuous movement, and approves stability, while it detects limping measures and rejects those that are excessive and extravagant.
—**Quintilian,** *Institutio Oratorio, vol. 3*

by two unstressed syllables (' - -). Examples would be strawberry and murmuring. Mark the dactyls in this following example from Dryden.

> After the pangs of a desperate lover,
> When day and night I have sighed all in vain,
> Ah what a pleasure it is to discover
> In her eyes pity, who causes my pain.

To review, simply get these basic cadences into the mind.

Basic cadences

> Iambic: daDUM daDUM daDUM daDUM
> Trochaic: DAduh DAduh DAduh DAduh
> Anapestic: dadaDUM dadaDUM dadaDUM dadaDUM
> Dactylic: DAduhduh DAduhduh DAduhduh DAduhduh

What is a metrical line? A metrical line is a line with a certain number of feet. Each line above, for example, has four feet. For our purposes now, such a line with four feet is called tetrameter. A line with five feet is called pentameter. Now it is important to note that these terms refer to the number of feet a line has but not to the kind of feet that line has. Thus, a line of poetry could be iambic pentameter, or it could be dactylic tetrameter. Or, if the poet felt like it, they could be dactylic pentameter or iambic tetrameter. Any of the different kinds of feet can be found in any of the different kinds of metrical line.

What is an example of tetrameter? Remember that a line of tetrameter poetry has four feet in it. In the portion of the poem considered earlier, the first and third lines were iambic tetrameter. Another example is "O for a thousand tongues to sing."

What is pentameter? A line of pentameter has five feet in it. One of the more common metrical lines in English poetry is iambic pentameter, which this short epigram from Alexander Pope illustrates (partially).

> You beat your pate, and fancy wit will come:
> Knock as you please, there's nobody at home.

Now we are almost there. What is rhyme? Rhyme occurs when there is a likeness or similarity in the sounds of two words. Not surprisingly, there are differences in various kinds of rhyme, but we are speaking here of true rhyme. This occurs when two syllables are equally stressed and sound identical, although the letters preceding those rhyming vowel sounds are different. Thus *bun* and *gun* constitute a true rhyme, because the vowel sounds of the syllables are identical, and they are preceded by differing consonants.

What are the different kinds of rhyme? The different kinds of rhyme are masculine rhyme, feminine (or double) rhyme, and triple rhyme. Masculine rhyme occurs when one syllable of a word rhymes with another word. Examples of this are easy to find and abound in bad poetry—moon and June, tight and light, sun and fun. Feminine rhyme, or double rhyme, occurs when the last two syllables of a word rhyme with two other syllables. Examples would be battle and cattle, or lighten and brighten. Triple rhyme is found when the last three syllables of a word or line rhyme with another three syllables.

> Like a river glorious
> Is God's perfect peace,
> Over all victorious
> In its bright increase

What is a rhyme scheme? A rhyme scheme is the sequence or pattern of rhyme in a poem. A rhyme scheme is usually represented through a notation of letters. The first end sound is designated as *a*, with the second end sound designated as *b*, and so forth. When the line that rhymes with *a* arrives, it is also designated as *a*. The same thing goes for *b*, and on through the poem. The rhyme scheme is usually set off to the right of the poem. Keep in mind that different kinds of poems have different kinds of designated rhyme schemes.

> Jerusalem left standing stones   a
> Behind her when she fell forlorn,   b
> But in the temple grasping groans   a

relinquished faith in buried bones   a
And Christendom was born   b

Now fulfillment of your assignment means that you are going to have to sort through these various elements, combine and recombine until, hey, an English sonnet enters the world.

So what is a sonnet? A sonnet is a poem consisting of fourteen lines of iambic pentameter. There are two important forms of the sonnet, the Italian (or Petrarchan) and the English (or Shakespearean).

What is the Italian sonnet? An Italian or Petrarchan sonnet has fourteen lines, an eight-line octave and a six-line sestet. The octave has a rhyme scheme of a-b-b-a-a-b-b-a. The sestet can have several different rhyme schemes, either c-d-e-c-d-e or c-d-c-d-c-d. The octave presents a problem or makes some kind of statement, while the sestet will summarize or give a solution to the problem presented. This is mentioned simply so you do not accidentally write an Italian sonnet.

So here is your concern, the English sonnet. An English or Shakespearean sonnet has fourteen lines, consisting of three quatrains followed by a concluding couplet. The rhyme scheme is a-b-a-b-c-d-c-d-e-f-e-f-g-g.

In our remaining space, we will consider three aspects of writing your sonnet, followed by two answers for those who have nothing better to do than carp at your noble efforts to recover a poetic soul.

But the thing you must know, that which you must grasp, is that an English sonnet is a particular thing, like a carburetor in a '92 Ford. If you would write one, that which you write must have those constituent elements. And before you can learn to do it well, you have to learn to do it.

You will discover, as you write, that you will frequently have to write your sentences backwards. The last word in each line is more anchored than the others, and this means that it is frequently helpful to start there.

Secondly, get the rhythms into your head. This week that rhythm is daDUMdaDUMdaDUM, which you will not accent in this way when you read the poetry, in the interest of avoiding sing-songy painfulness, but nevertheless this is the skeletal structure that must be there. It may be helpful to try to speak iambic to your roommate. "I think that I shall never call my folks when you tie up the phone like this. Besides, the dinner dishes wait and call for you; they wail and moan. They cry, O when, O when shall we be clean?"

And third, whatever you do, avoid clichés like the plague. Um, avoid clichés like . . . a bad thing to be avoided.

But what then are we to make of those stout fellows who think that writing sonnets is, at best, the relic of another age and at worst, the carrier of all the worst forms of moon/Juning that afflict the soul of every sensitive man?

The first thing we must do is refute through example. In your rhyming, stay away from trite or clichéd rhymes. As you follow the meter, do not thump like an amplified metronome. In your sentiments, do not write of that which inspires Hallmark poets everywhere. Do not attempt to pry open your ribcage and flash passersby with your sadly beating little heart.

A second refutation is to point to the universal and metrical history of mankind, the last one hundred years excepted. Poetry has existed, literally, from the first split moment of time. So what do your video-gaming friends know?

In summary, we have considered what poetry is, and we have defined the constituent elements of poetry—at least the kind of poetry that concerns us here. These elements of poetry, not surprisingly, are also found as making up the form of poetry known as the English sonnet. There are pitfalls, we acknowledge them gladly, and we have anticipated and answered the more obvious objections. But recall Chesterton's dictum, which is that before you can learn to do something well, you have to learn to do it badly.

> I do not neglect clausular rhythm in my own speaking, but apply it in what I consider to be moderation; and in our writers they have extra appeal because I find them so rarely.
>
> —**Saint Augustine,** *On Christian Teaching*

SUGGESTED READING

1. Aristotle, *Rhetoric*, II.XXIV.1—XXV.14
2. Quintilian, *Institutio Oratoria*, vol. 3, IX.III.16—IV.41

EXERCISE

1. Write three English sonnets. Present the best one publicly.

REVIEW QUESTIONS

1. What is poetry?
2. What is meter?
3. What is a foot?
4. What is an iamb?
5. What is a trochee?
6. What is an anapest?
7. What is a dactyl?
8. What is tetrameter?
9. What is pentameter?
10. Pick three of the quoted portions of poetry in this chapter, and discuss the meter exhibited in them.
11. What is masculine rhyme? Feminine?
12. How is a rhyme scheme identified?
13. How can meter be utilized in a prose oration? What is to be avoided?
14. Prepare five couplets of poetry of your own composing, using different meters. Present them, and afterwards be prepared to point out some of your metrical devices.

The Rhythm of Words: 2

Think about this for a moment. The meter of your prose is as present as the meter of your poetry. The difference is that the meter of your poetry is identified and set apart, while the meter of your prose meanders and hides (occasionally under bushels). Nevertheless, at least a portion of your ear should be attuned to this aspect of your supposedly mundane talk.

When you consider the "rhythm of words," there are at least two aspects of that rhythm which must be kept in mind. We have already considered the first—the question of overt rhythm and meter. But take care to remember the second, which we might call "thought rhymes and meter."

If you pay no attention, like we are doing here, to your thought meter, so to speak, then the end result, which is obvious if you think about it, is to yank the listener around on the end of a rope, which is not what you wanted really. The sentence is disjointed and hobbles around looking for its cane. But if you pay close attention, and treat your listener with courtesy, then the effect is far more pleasing to the ear and eye. Now go back to our original paragraph. What occurreth there? Go through the paragraph and try to note the metrical elements woven through it. For example, the first sentence is two dactyls and a trochee—DAduhduh DAduhduh DAduh. *Think about this for a moment.*

> Well, you ask, is an orator then always to speak as he writes? If possible, always.
> —**Quintilian**, *Institutio Oratorio, vol. 4*

The meter of your prose is as present as the meter of your poetry. The difference is that the meter of your poetry is identified and set apart, while the meter of your prose meanders and hides (occasionally under bushels). Nevertheless, at least a portion of your ear should be attuned to this aspect of your supposedly mundane talk.

We have seen the basic metrical structures of poetry. We have now seen that these structures do not appear in poetry and evaporate in prose. They are equally present in both but function with different goals in mind.

It should be obvious by now that meter is inescapable. We hope that by the time we are done, you will see the difference it can make for your prose if you embrace that inescapable reality and learn to tinker with it. As for those who object to the entire procedure, we may spend a few minutes dealing with their objections.

Of course, the public speaker should not try to turn his prose into metrical poetry. But he should use what he knows of metered poetry, scattering that knowledge throughout. In other words, do not speak trochaic, but use trochees. Do not speak iambic, but use iambs. That's the idea. If poetry is concentrated language, then think of prose as poetry spread out. Good prose is like old wine, diluted with wisdom. But, to change the metaphor, we do not take a homeopathic approach.

For a sample confirmatio, let us consider a series of triplets. One mangled or mundane, one poetic, one a more mature prose.

1. Bob went to the store.
2. And Robert thought that he could go; he thought to bring the groceries home.
3. Empty, hungry, Robert stepped outside and into sideways morning light.

1. Do not think to stop the inevitable.
2. It comes, it surely comes—how can mortal man withstand it?
3. The inevitable comes, and he who thinks to stop it is surely misguided.

1. This class meets on Monday.
2. The dedicated day (Monday) has come; the students settle in their seats.
3. Monday comes and lecture always rides it.

Shall we follow the example of those painters whose sole aim is to be able to copy pictures by using the ruler and the measuring rod?
—Quintilian, *Institutio Oratorio, vol. 4*

Think about the contexts and goals for each of these triplets. Which one accomplishes the goal most effectively. The answer? Number 3 wins out of the first group. Of the second group, which sentence best communicates a fatalistic sense of the inevitable. Number 1. And, out of the final group, which is the one that is most likely to help you remember when lecture is four weeks from now. Number 3.

Now the charge that can be brought against speaking this way is that it is entirely too artificial—words trying to function simultaneously on stilts and steroids. The answer is that we are certainly not trying to turn prose into poetry. The rhythms of a creek chattering down a mountainside are quite different from the rhythms of an irrigation ditch. Or, if we wanted a comparison more favorable to poetry, the rhythms of a free brook are different than a watered Persian garden. Both have their pattern; both have a rhythm. And some of these things they have in common.

If I had thought to write and speak, in all I do and all I say, in metered form which cannot say its selfsame name, because the name it somehow bears, is not the form it represents, I could not go for two lines more without the hearers writhing in their seats.

But a judicious use of iambs has a completely different effect. It only brings pure thoughts to mind; it cures a pestilential brain.

Now, at the end of the day, you may feel like the writer who was so exhausted—he spent all morning putting in a comma and all afternoon taking it out. But no matter. Life's tough all 'round. Deal with it.

As the aspiring speaker learns to do this, he will find that larger patterns can emerge. He will use short bursts of iambs, or a longer chain of dactyls, and he will vary how he uses them. If you are that aspiring speaker, do not be afraid to use them, and do not be afraid to experiment with them awkwardly. Write a paragraph, and then rewrite it so that it has at least two intervals of anapestic joy and happiness. Then play around with trochees some, although I did not do that here. Iambs call you, let them come. Roll around in words like they were autumn leaves. Sprinkle them over the top of your head.

SUGGESTED READING

1. Aristotle, *Rhetoric*, II.XXVI.I—III.II.IO

2. Quintilian, *Institutio Oratoria*, vol. 3, IX.IV.42—IV.147

EXERCISE

1. Take a 250 word selection of your own descriptive prose. Go through and identify any metric bursts that may already be present. Edit the rest, rewriting sections to include samples of each of the four types of meter. Try to do it in such a way that the piece improves. Present publicly.

REVIEW QUESTIONS

1. What is poetry?
2. What is prose?
3. How can prose use iambs without being iambic?

Still More Rhythm of Words

The concept of all this is easy enough to grasp, but learning to do it is quite another thing. For that, what is called for is practice, practice, practice. And what is the underlined line? Trochee, trochee, trochee. Pay attention in this chapter, underlining and identifying any phrases that have a consistent meter.

As you no doubt recall, the basic forms of meter are these: an iambic foot (or an iamb) is a two-syllable word, or two syllables in a row, with the stress on the second syllable. The iamb is the most common foot in English poetry, and looks like this (- ').

Beside the stream I thought to rest,
I thought to rest and wait for light.

A trochaic foot (or a trochee) is a two-syllable word, or two syllables in a row, in which the stress comes first (' -).

Once I thought to keep my backpack,
once I thought to eat my lunch.

Or consider how to modify our iambic example:

And beside the stream I thought a while . . .

An anapestic foot (or an anapest) is a three-syllable word, or three syllables in a row, consisting of two unstressed syllables followed by a stressed syllable (- - ').

Eloquence is like a harp and will never reach perfection, unless all its strings be taut and in tune.
—**Quintilian**, *Institutio Oratorio, vol. 2*

And we saw that the candle which flickered at night . . .

A dactylic foot (or a dactyl) is a three-syllable word, or three syllables in a row, consisting of a stressed syllable followed by two unstressed syllables (' - -).

Stand by the water and listen for dangers,
  walk by the water and listen in fear.

A metrical line is a line with a certain number of feet. A line with four feet is called tetrameter. A line with five feet is called pentameter.

We have covered (again) the definitions of the basic forms of meter, and in our argument we are simply going over them again in order to give you the practice you certainly need.

Knowledge should not be thought of as an abstraction—knowledge is doing. This means that an essential part of poetic knowledge is to feel it in your bones—and give your speech while standing on the balls of your feet.

Remember that you are not trying to write pure poetry—this is a speech in pedestrian prose and you do need some roughage.

1. Talk about it. Try to decide maybe.
2. Talk about the issue first, and then perhaps you might decide.

1. The president's speech to Congress was okay.
2. The presidential foray to the Hill was for the most part well-received.

1. The bus driver was upset.
2. The driver of the bus heaped anger upon anger.

No new information here. Practice is essential. We are simply trying to prepare you for your new life as a rhetor.

A speaker who clarifies something that needs to be learnt is a blessing, but a speaker who labors things already learnt is a bore.
—**Saint Augustine,** *On Christian Teaching*

SUGGESTED READING

1. Aristotle, *Rhetoric*, III.II.II—IV.4
2. Quintilian, *Institutio Oratoria*, vol. 4, X.I.I—X.I.107

EXERCISE

1. Pick a topic and write an exordium (250–300 words) for an imaginary composition. Use all four types of meter as often as you can without the rhythm becoming too overt (and horrible). Present publicly.

REVIEW QUESTIONS

1. Give three examples of iambic words.
2. Give three examples of trochaic words.
3. Give three examples of anapestic words.
4. Give three examples of dactylic words.
5. Write a letter to the editor that you agree with (obviously), but your main point in doing it is to write a letter that has some metrical life to it.

LESSON 25

Metaphor and Style

We have already noted that style is not an afterthought, sprinkled on top of an otherwise insipid oration. Your style is an essential part of your oration—your style is woven throughout your ethos, pathos, and logos. But this, to be rightly understood, has to be understood down at the foundation. Style is not to be sprinkled on top of your talk like so many M&Ms on top of your frozen yogurt.

The universe is a figure of speech. And, now that I have your attention, allow me to explain first what I do not mean. The modernist and the postmodernist agree on one essential thing—that metaphor is meaningless. The modernist therefore seeks meaning in brute factuality, the objectivist view of scientific materialism. The postmodernist grants that metaphor is meaningless but then wants to go on to say that everything is metaphor. Putting this together, we see that he is saying that everything is meaningless (except for him talking about it, but we weren't giving him government grants to be consistent).

Now, when we say that "everything is metaphor," conservative Christians attuned to the nuances of the threat posed by postmodernism tend to blurt an *uh oh*. But they are leaving out half the sentence, which, in this case, happens to be the most important half.

God created the heavens and the earth through the Word. God sustains and holds together the heavens and earth through the Word. The universe is God speaking. Everything that is, is a visible word. And even more specifically, the Word and sacraments follow. These are not examples of God speaking when He was otherwise silent. They are examples of God speaking in a clear manner so that we might come to understand how He has spoken in and through everything else.

Style has three kinds of excellence, correctness, lucidity, and elegance.
—**Quintilian,** *Institutio Oratorio, vol. 1*

Now the Bible says that the created order speaks about God. But it speaks precisely because it is spoken. The universe speaks, not as the source of knowledge, but speaks as our words, for example, "speak" about us.

What follows? Everything created reveals something about the Creator. Everything is a simile. If the created order reflects the glory of God, and, if every aspect of it does, then we can rejoice in the fact. But after we have done this, we should push on into new territory. How does the created order glorify God? It does so through being like Him. In some way, in some respect, everything is a simile.

All things are therefore cognates. And you should look for them. The affinities are there. If *a* is like *A* in the Creator and *b* is like *B* in the Creator, and so on, what follows? *A* and *B* and *C* within the Godhead are all internally consistent. This means that all things in the universe (*a* and *b* and so on) are all cousins. And this is what makes effective metaphor possible.

What else follows? The reformational view of things is much more the poet as "seer," as opposed to the poet as maker. What he sees are the interconnections between apparently disparate things, but the interconnections are built-in. The striking metaphor does not tie two isolated things together but rather reveals a similarity initially spoken by God, and then seen and declared by us. This does not mean anything can relate in any way to any other thing. It has to relate in the way God made the world.

The foundation of all of this is found in the way God is. In the beginning was the Word—*en arche en ho Logos.*

A metaphor is that which is fully identified with something distinct from itself. Not only may a metaphor communicate truth, it is the only thing which can do so. This means that a Christian speaker has to understand the Word before he can hope to work effectively with words.

The Word of God is not a metaphor in the sense that we derive our understanding of Him from studying our words. Rather, the ultimate Word is that from which every word spoken by every creature, whether spoken in heaven or on earth, derives its name.

A metaphor must not be too great for its subject or, as is more frequently the case, too little, and that it must not be inappropriate.
—**Quintilian,** *Institutio Oratorio, vol. 3*

We begin with an ultimate metaphor. In the first place, at the *arche*, in the place of preeminence, at the place where all things cohere, was the Word. The Word was with God, and the Word was God. That is, the Word is God completely, and, at the same time, the Word is distinct from God in the sense that we are able to say He is "with" God. The Son is God, but the Son is not the Father.

Now between God the Speaker and God the Spoken, there is no degradation of meaning. The Word does not obscure meaning but rather reveals it. This is a revelation of love. The connection between God the Speaker and God the Spoken is not a matter of mere data transfer. The Father and Son love one another with an everlasting love. This love is Himself a Person, the Holy Spirit of God, the Holy Spirit of the Word.

Thus, the Father speaks the Word in love, and the Word spoken reveals the Father in love. This is the unifying Spirit of love, the Spirit who is the reason why there is no degradation of meaning. How could there be? The divine hermeneutic is therefore the Holy Spirit. He searches the deep things of God. The ultimate hermeneutic is therefore a divine Person.

The Word spoken by God is not a solitary word—neither a lonely monistic noun nor a verb in the flux of any created temporal process. Yet the Son is eternally begotten, the Word is eternally spoken, the Light eternally shines. Thus the Word contains within Himself all the wisdom of the Godhead. The Word is therefore the Metaphor of God.

Not surprisingly, the way God is affects the creation He spoke into being. God spoke the created universe into being. God the Father "God-the-Son-ed" light, and there was light. God the Speaker Worded the heavens and the earth, and so they came to be.

But God did not need to create the universe in order to speak the Word. The Son was eternally begotten by the Father. The Word was eternally spoken by the Father without dependence on any aspect of the creative decree. The creation did not bring the triune nature of God into being. Nevertheless, when God in the good pleasure of His will determined to create the heavens and earth, it was fitting and necessary that God speak the universe into existence through His organ of speech, that is to say, the Word. Without Him was not anything made that was made.

As the Father speaks the Word in love, so the Word spoken speaks in turn about the Father in love. As the Word, in love, spoke the creation into being, so the creation speaks about the Word in love. And so the heavens declare the glory of God. The universe is therefore a metaphor of the Word of God and faithfully reveals Him. Day after day pours forth speech.

Man was created in the image of this speaking, self-revealing God. Man is therefore created in the image of God the Speaker, God the Spoken, and God the Interpreter. In the first place, therefore, the word was with man and the word was man, and a spirit of love bound the two together.

God gave this man dominion in the earth and commissioned him with the authority of naming. Whenever a man lawfully names, he is exercising the authority of covenant naming and is doing so as a covenant head and lord. What is man that you are mindful of him? Whenever a man names, he reveals himself.

When a man names lawfully, that which he names becomes that thing—this is true in history, in literature, in science, and art. Adam had the authority to name the animals, and Eve. Eve had the authority to name her children. Since the creation of our first parents, we have never stopped naming.

Naming lawfully is dependent upon a hermeneutic of humility. A word has fuller meaning within the context of a sentence; a sentence has fuller meaning within the context of a story, and a story has fuller meaning within the context of a worldview. In order to name rightly, a man must therefore have the worldview God requires of him.

Because man has fallen, his redemption must include the redemption of metaphor. Since the Fall, when a man names, he reveals himself as a sinner. He is a fallen lord, a fallen namer. His words therefore obscure meaning, not because they are words, but because they proceed from a lying heart. The Word took on flesh and dwelt among us. The Incarnation of the Word was directed to the restoration of words. This is why the Scriptures place such importance on preaching and on the sacraments.

There is no degradation of meaning at the ultimate place of metaphor—the Trinity. The Word is distinct from the Father and yet fully identified with Him. Because of this, we have a basis for confidence in our own faithful use of metaphor.

A man's words reveal, first, the man. The words are not the man, and yet they reveal him faithfully and are to be identified with him. Out of the abundance of the heart, the man speaks. The foundational nature of all language is therefore metaphorical because every word a man speaks reveals himself—just as God reveals Himself through the Word. Every word spoken ultimately reveals the speaker.

The secondary nature of metaphor is seen as man images God as creator through sub-creation. Words that a man speaks may therefore reveal other words a man speaks. A man speaks of one thing in terms of another—my love is a red, red rose. This is our ordinary use of the word metaphor. This ordinary use does not explain everything; rather, it needs to be explained by everything.

Every word is a metaphor. A metaphor is that which is distinct from that which it names, but it nevertheless fully identifies with that which it names. Smoke means fire as a sign. The word *smoke* means smoke as a symbol and functions in a triadic fashion.

The issue is therefore not your creativity, but rather you being trained in what to look for. It is there—but what is the shape of the leaf?

Now—training the eye. Just a few thoughts:

Learn the metaphors and figures of Scripture.

Look to the metaphors and figures of the natural world.

Note the metaphors and figures of history.

Immerse yourself in the metaphors and figures of literature and allusion.

> For a speech which is out of keeping with the man who delivers it is just as faulty as the speech which fails to suit the subject to which it should conform.
> —**Quintilian,** *Institutio Oratorio, vol. 3*

> Embellishment we use in order to adorn and enrich the argument, after the Proof has been established.
> —*Rhetorica Ad Herennium*

SUGGESTED READING

1. Aristotle, *Rhetoric,* III.V.I—IX.3

2. *Rhetorica Ad Herennium,* IV.XX.27—IV.XXXII.44

3. Quintilian, *Institutio Oratoria,* vol. 4, X.I.108—VI.7

EXERCISE

I. Find a striking visual scene in the world around you and write a 250–300 word description of it for a blind man. Do not drift into an action blow-by-blow, and do not appeal to the sense he does not have. Trans-sensual metaphor is your friend. Present publicly.

REVIEW QUESTIONS

1. What is style not to be considered as?
2. In what way is the universe a figure of speech?
3. Why are all things cognates?
4. How is this a foundation for metaphor?
5. If the Father speaks, and the Son is the spoken Word, then what is the correct interpretation?

LESSON 26

Indirect Information

Our interest now is in the selection and use of words, particularly words that carry metaphorical freight, which is to say, most of them.

Whenever we are called upon to justify what we do down here on earth, our first instinct should always be to look to Scripture, and we must do this more broadly than we are accustomed to doing. If metaphor is just sprinkled on top of our discourse, then our choices are simple. We may refuse to do it, leaving our discourse plain and unvarnished. Or we may sprinkle heavily, opting for sophism.

But recall who God is—the Son reveals the Father perfectly, without anything breaking down.

Remember the hypostatic union—the glorious incarnation brings two utterly unlike things (Deity and humanity) together in perfect harmony. This is an ultimate justification for metaphorical juxtaposition. Recall the doctrine of creation through the Word—the universe is God speaking. We are invited to search the world for indicators of ultimate meaning.

After the previous chapter, let us attempt to come down to earth. The theology of the thing is well and good, and most necessary. But you still need to know how to proceed. The first thing is to lose certain common assumptions about the Scriptures—these assumptions keep the Scriptures from doing their intended work in the soul.

A certain turn of (unpoetic) mind is unhappily literal. This has always been the case, but over the last century or so, a certain school of hermeneutical interpretation has turned this failure of soul into an interpretative virtue. Thus, the Scripture is interpreted "literally," as opposed, for example, to what liberals do with it. But this is a false contrast.

To call this the Swollen style will prove correct. For just as a swelling often resembles a healthy condition of the body, so, to those who are inexperienced, turgid and inflated language often seems majestic—when a thought is expressed either in new or archaic words, or in clumsy metaphors, or in diction more impressive than the theme demands.
—*Rhetorica Ad Herennium*

129

When we begin to read the Bible with greater depth and richness, objections crowd into our minds. We suspect we are in the backseat of an out-of-control car, and we want to know where the brakes are. But this is a question that confronts us with every method of interpretation, including detailed word studies. We must reject a strip-mining approach to exegesis.

For instance, in Matthew 16, Jesus answers those who say they want a sign. He says no sign will be given except the sign of *Jonah*. A little later in the chapter, Peter confesses that Jesus is the Christ. Jesus pronounces a tremendous blessing on him—on Simon, son of Jonah. A little later, Peter pulls a Jonah and rebukes Jesus for His prediction that He will spend three days and three nights in the heart of the earth, thus fulfilling the sign of Jonah. The apostle argued with the Lord, just as the prophet did.

Fascinating, but we still want to stay closer to shore. We simply want to know that something is the direct object here because it is in the accusative case and in the same sentence.

It is important to read carefully and broadly. In the last chapter, we said that the reader should ransack Scripture for its figures and metaphors. What else, you might wonder. Actually, this will take you the rest of your life, and the task is not as narrow as you might think.

Picture the main street of a desolate Western town, midday, one hundred and fifty years ago. The street is deserted, except for a few blowing tumbleweeds. Some townspeople are looking out of the windows of the shops. Now, what is about to happen? And how do you know this? This is a particular motif, with which we are familiar. You know what's about to happen. You can even hear the spurs jingling on a wooden sidewalk. A spiny castle on a mountainside at dusk, complete with crescent moon and fluttering bats communicates just as quickly.

Now picture a man dressed in a biblical manner. He is standing next to a well. In the distance, a woman is approaching with a jar on her shoulder. What is going to happen? Now, what is the meaning of Christ's encounter with the Samaritan woman? His Father is seeking worshipers, that is to say, a bride for His Son. Are you surprised that His disciples were flustered? They knew the stories; they knew what went

For it is a better exercise for the memory to learn the words of others than it is to learn one's own.
—**Quintilian,** *Institutio Oratorio, vol. 2*

down at wells—matchmaking—and they could spot it as easily as you can spot a pending gunfight.

We need to learn how to see when *this* is *that.* Let your speech be gravid with metaphor.

SUGGESTED READING

1. Aristotle, *Rhetoric,* III.IX.4—X.7
2. *Rhetorica Ad Herennium,* IV.XXXIII.44—IV.LVI.69
3. Quintilian, *Institutio Oratoria,* vol. 4, X.VII.I—XI.I.78

EXERCISE

1. Write three short paragraphs. In each one you do nothing other than set the stage. When you are done setting the stage, describing as fully as you can, read what you have publicly. Have your audience write down their guesses as to what will happen next. Try to make the scenery and the setting; write the next lines of dialog in your play.

REVIEW QUESTIONS

1. What is a motif?
2. How does a motif communicate?
3. What was ironic about Christ's use of the sign of Jonah?
4. If someone demanded proof that a Western scene was preliminary to a gunfight, how could you provide that proof?

Style and Reading

We are going to begin with the obvious, or with what should be obvious, once it is pointed out. Recall for a moment what Quintillian wanted for a child's nurse. We learn to speak in the first place by imitation, and if the student grows up in an environment festooned with solecisms, he will come to hear his first born saying that "Me and her wanna go to the park." This principle does not change as you grow older. A man's reading and his company will shape his discourse. Now, as always, bad companions corrupt more than good morals.

For my own part, I regard clearness as the first essential of a good style.
—**Quintilian,** *Institutio Oratorio, vol. 3*

Consider the stylistic strengths of some of the following writers, with H. L. Mencken coming first.

No rational man can go through the endless volumes of the Loeb Library without concluding that the Romans were an essentially dull and practical people, without much more fancy in them than a Congressman or a cow doctor. They had their high virtues, of course, but a lush and charming imagination was certainly not one.[1]

This incredible work is an almost inexhaustible mine of bad writing, faulty generalizing, childish pussyfooting, ludicrous posturing, and naive stupidity. To find a match for it one must try to imagine a biography of the Duke of Wellington by his barber.[2]

Self-respect—The secure feeling that no one, as yet, is suspicious.[3]

1. "Classical Learning," from *A Mencken Chrestomathy,* (New York: Vintage Books, [1949] 1982), 312.
2. "Consolation," *The Smart Set,* vol. 64, issue 1 (Jan. 1921): 142.
3. "Sententiae" from *The Vintage Mencken* (Hadley Press, 2008), 231.

Another master of style was C. S. Lewis.

> A tree grows because it adds rings: a train doesn't grow by leaving one station behind and puffing on to the next.[4]

> For famished nature will be avenged and a hard heart is no infallible protection against a soft head.[5]

> Anger is the fluid that love bleeds when you cut it.[6]

One of Lewis's friends was J. R. R. Tolkien.

> So deadly and ineluctable is the underlying thought, that those who in the circle of light, within the besieged hall, are absorbed in work or talk and do not look to the battlements, either do not regard it or recoil. Death comes to the feast, and they say He gibbers: He has no sense of proportion.[7]

> "All right, all right!" said Sam. "That's quite enough. I don't want to hear no more. No welcome, no beer, no smoke, and a lot of rules and orc-talk instead."[8]

P. J. O' Rourke also has some great moments.

> American embassies, too, are all over the map and always breathtaking. In the middle of London, on beautiful Grosvenor Square, there's one that looks like a bronzed Oldsmobile dashboard. And rising from the slums of Manila is another that resembles the Margarine of the Future Pavilion at the 1959 Brussels World Fair. I assume this is all the work of one architect, and I assume he's on drugs.[9]

4. *Of Other Worlds* (San Diego: Harcourt, 2002), 26.
5. *The Abolition of Man* (New York: HarperCollins, [1944] 2001), 14.
6. *Letters to Malcolm* (San Diego: Harcout, 1992), 97.
7. *The Monsters & the Critics* (London: HarperCollins, 1983), 19.
8. *The Return of the King* (New York: Houghton Mifflin Company, 1955), 977.
9. *Holidays in Hell* (New York: Grove Press: 2000), 10.

The great cynic of the nineteenth century, Ambrose Bierce, has a lot to show us as well.

> Erudition, n. Dust shaken out of a book into an empty skull.[10]

> Esophagus, n. That portion of the alimentary canal that lies between pleasure and business.[11]

> Exhort, v.t. In religious affairs, to put the conscience of another upon the spit and roast it to a nut brown discomfort.[12]

> Mouth, n. In man, the gateway to the soul; in woman, the outlet of the heart.[13]

One of the stylistic masters was G. K. Chesterton.

> They are aesthetes; and the definition of an aesthete is a man who is experienced enough to admire a good picture, but not inexperienced enough to see it.[14]

> He curses the Sultan because Christian girls lose their virginity, and then curses Mrs. Grundy because they keep it. As a politician, he will cry out that war is a waste of life, and then, as a philosopher, that all life is a waste of time.[15]

> If you really want poor children to go to the seaside, you cannot think it illiberal that they should go there on flying dragons; you can only think it unlikely.[16]

> The theology behind classic style does not admit that there is anything that counts as truth that cannot be presented briefly and memorably.
> —**Francis-Noel Thomas and Mark Turner,** *Clear and Simple as the Truth*

10. *The Enlarged Devil's Dictionary* (London: Penguin, 1967), 113.
11. Ibid., 113.
12. Ibid., 118.
13. Ibid., 228.
14. *Lunacy and Letters* (New York: Sheed and Ward, 1958), 92.
15. *Orthodoxy* (New York: Doubleday Dell, 1959), 41.
16. Ibid., 127.

What is the point of such extended quotations? You should fill a commonplace book with pages and pages of quotes like these and better. You should taste them, dissect them, improve them, and compete with them. Read, and then read some more. Read good stuff. Read people who handle the language well. Write down good stuff you find. Tinker with it. Move things around. Filch parts of it. Change the adjectives while keeping the contrast. Quote them. Let them shape your head. And, as Grace Slick put it, feed your head.

SUGGESTED READING

1. Aristotle, *Rhetoric*, III.XI.I—XII.3
2. *Rhetorica Ad Herennium*, IV.I.I—IV.X.15
3. Quintilian, *Institutio Oratoria*, vol. II.I.79—III.32

EXERCISE

1. Choose one of the quotations above (or an example of excellence from your own commonplace book). Shoplift it as an opening line or paragraph for a short argumentative piece. Add 250 words to its back-end, attempting to match its tone, beat, and voice. Present publicly.

REVIEW QUESTIONS

It is scarcely possible to say how much more readily we imitate those whom we like.
—**Quintilian,** *Institutio Oratorio, vol. 1*

1. What is the importance of imitation in learning how to speak well?
2. What did Quintilian set great importance on for this reason?
3. Out of the quotations listed in this chapter, which was your favorite? Why?
4. Which was your least favorite? Why?

Elocution

The end is near. Finishing touches must come out and play. Elocution is the art of speaking distinctly, clearly, and well with regard to the pronunciation and relations of your words, as opposed to making the kind of sound a man makes when he is trying to speak through his wooly muffler. In this, as always, remember that it is art to conceal art. Elocution is at the center of delivery.

Elocution has certain components: quality, force, pitch, movement, stress, and intervals. The words themselves will carry some of this, but do not expect them to do all the work.

First is the matter of *quality*. Under this head, think of quality as the character of sound or timbre of your voice. If your voice were a musical instrument, which instrument would it be? And then, having determined that, ask what range of musical possibilities does this instrument have?

Then there is *force*. The force of enunciation can range from impassioned down to laid back. Force can be understood as the variation of strength and weakness. The voice can speak softly, pianissimo, and go on up to fortissimo. When this kind of range is employed in parts of the speaking, we would think of it under the heading of stress.

What about *pitch?* Where a person sings in the choir can help determine where he is likely to be in his speaking. And believe it or not, pitch is an important part of oratory. The main thing, in most occasions that are likely to be encountered, is to keep the pitch variations from being like a roller coaster ride at Six Flags Over Georgia.

Not surprisingly, *movement* refers to whether or not you speak quickly or slowly.

For clearness is the first virtue of eloquence, and the less talented a man is, the more he will strive to exalt and dilate himself, just as short men tend to walk on tip-toe and weak men to use threats.
—**Quintilian,** *Institutio Oratorio, vol. 1*

The second essential is variety of tone, and it is in this alone that delivery really consists.
—**Quintilian,** *Institutio Oratorio, vol. 4*

But although words must be given their full phonetic value, it is a tiresome and offensive trick to pronounce every letter as if we were entering them in an inventory.
—**Quintilian,** *Institutio Oratorio, vol. 4*

With *stress*, what is emphasized? The beginnings of words, the ends of them, or those vowels in the middle? Probably the simplest way to describe this is to speak of it in terms of vowel-speakers and consonant-speakers. Those who have a drawl are vowel-speakers and those who speak in a quick, clipped fashion tend to be consonant-speakers.

What about *intervals?* The questions answered here are, "Where do you pause? How long do you pause?" And does the speaker pause simply because he ran out of air, or was there thought behind it?

Suppose for a moment a speaker wanted to express sorrow, or simple narrative, or wrath. And in doing this remember that each speaker is operating from a different baseline—each has a different kind of voice.

Suppose the task is to say the following line. Before delivering it, mark some suggestions in each of the categories.

"Oh, the deep soul it breathed! The love, the woe, the fervor, poured out in that song!"

SORROW

Quality: _____

Force: _____

Pitch: _____

Movement: _____

Stress: _____

Intervals: _____

"Cindy bought a brown mare for her daughter."

STORY

Quality: _____

Force: _____

Pitch: _____

Movement: _____

Stress: _____

Intervals: _____

"Had all his hairs been lives, my great revenge had stomach for them all."

WRATH

Quality: _____

Force: _____

Pitch: _____

Movement: _____

Stress: _____

Intervals: _____

For my part, I should not readily say that any one of the five faculties is the most important; that an exceptionally great usefulness resides in the delivery I should boldly affirm.

—*Rhetorica Ad Herrennium*

SUGGESTED READING

1. Aristotle, *Rhetoric*, III.XII.4—XIV.12
2. *Rhetorica Ad Herennium*, IV.XI.16—IV.XIX.27
3. Quintilian, *Institutio Oratoria*, vol. 4, II.III.33—III.160

EXERCISES

1. Find an angry rant and attempt to deliver it as lighthearted humor through modifying the above elements.
2. Added difficulty: Place an oddly-shaped foreign object in your mouth (Lego, six mints, small piece of lemon, etc.) and attempt to deliver your chosen piece unaffected.

REVIEW QUESTIONS

1. What is the quality of a person's voice?
2. What does force mean?
3. What does pitch refer to?
4. What is the significance of movement in speaking?
5. What is stress in speech?
6. And what does interval refer to?

Stance and Gestures

If speaking in public is a "kind" of music, as we have already considered, then what is the instrument exactly? The easiest assumption to make (and a wrong one) is that the "instrument" is made up of the vocal chords and mouth. It is actually the whole body.

Modern technology introduces another series of issues which must be taken into account. The difference between a guitar and an electric guitar is considerable. In the same way, a preacher and an amplified preacher have to conduct themselves differently, if the technology is to be used and not to be a force which drives all before it. For example, everything is amplified and not just the good stuff. This means that George Whitefield, preaching to 30,000 people, without a microphone, could probably have afforded a little more throat-clearing and interesting nasal noises which a modern speaker cannot afford. These days such quirks are picked up via satellite and beamed all over the world.

At the same time, a number of things stay the same. First, let us consider posture and stance, working our way up from the floor. The two words you should consider here are disciplined and natural. Discipline means it should be thought through, and natural means a speaker should not scrunch himself up into a contrived little ball.

Feet should be approximately shoulder-width, evenly balanced. One foot can be slightly ahead of the other. The stance is warlike or athletic. And consequently, ladies should have their feet closer together, with one not ahead of the other. Unless your talk is "classroom informal," the speaker should stay that way for the duration of the talk, shifting the feet perhaps once. Even if he is behind a large lectern and thinks nobody will see or know what he is doing with his feet, the issue is what this does to the part of the body the words are coming from. If your talk

For the orator should be as unlike a dancer as possible, and his gesture should be adapted rather to his thought than to his actual words.
—**Quintilian**, *Institutio Oratorio, vol. 4*

141

is informal, then the speaker can stroll around the classroom, but if he does this, he needs to be in complete mastery of the material. He cannot get out to the end of his tether and realize that his next point is on the lectern, which is fifteen feet behind him.

The posture should be erect, with lots of opportunity for air to get down into your lungs. If a speaker huddles over his notes, he will not be able to breathe well. He must not use the lectern as a crutch. If he leans on it at all, then again the stance is one of "classroom informal." But even here, take care. Even if the posture itself is not unbecoming, it can affect the sounds issuing forth from your "instrument." You do not play your violin with a bent neck, or wouldn't, even if you could.

The eyes (and we are not here speaking of eye contact with the audience) need to be oriented to your immediate surroundings. The light there should be good so that it is possible to see the notes (if they are there). If the talk is completely extemp then this is not nearly as crucial. If the talk is being given in an unfamiliar place, it would be a good idea to stand for a moment where you are going to be speaking in order to get the lay of the land.

With regard to gesticulation, keep certain key principles in mind. Gestures, whatever they are, should underscore the point and not compete with it. Catalog those gestures (with the help of your eagle-eyed roommate) which are already natural. It will probably be a surprise to find out how many gestures are already native gestures, even if one is less Mediterranean in his ancestry than others perhaps are. Even if one is descended from frozen board Norwegian stock, certain gestures are still likely to be present. Decide which ones you can use while speaking and which of them you want to exclude—or which you want to exclude from certain parts of your talk.

As a general rule, do not juggle. If you are reading (say) from your manuscript, and you have to hold it, it would probably be safest to dispense with gesturing altogether. Unless, of course, you can use the manuscript itself in gesturing. Incidentally, holding a manuscript is not a good idea if nervousness is a problem. A manuscript is a great device for amplifying hand tremors so that even the people in back row can see them.

In fact, though the peoples and nations of the earth speak a multitude of tongues, they share in common the universal language of the hands.
—**Quintilian,** *Institutio Oratorio, vol. 4*

There are also times when a speaker must make a virtue of necessity. For example, taking glasses on and off can be used effectively—or be an insane distraction. Gestures can be used for emphasis, for example. Or they can be used to illustrate certain words. Or they can be used to reinforce a general pathos. In any case, they should not be just thrown in "just 'cause."

Learning new gestures raises the question of affectation. There is quite a difference between the awkwardness of learning something new on the one hand and affectation on the other. But remember that affectation is generally done well, although something is slightly "off." Also you should distinguish this from a growing persona.

Affectation is really a question of heart motive. Growing into a persona is an essential part of maturing. Anything you might choose to do is going to contribute to one persona or another. People will only call attention to it if it is markedly different from the course you were apparently on before. A persona, however, (coming full circle) should be disciplined and natural.

> Smite your hands together, stamp the ground, slap your thigh, your breast, your forehead, and you will go straight to the heart of the dingier members of your audience.
> —**Quintilian**, *Institutio Oratorio, vol. 1*

SUGGESTED READING

1. Aristotle, *Rhetoric*, III.XV.I—XVI.II
2. *Rhetorica Ad Herennium*, III.I.I—III.X.I8
3. Quintilian, *Institutio Oratoria*, vol. 4, II.III.I6I—XII.II.3I

EXERCISES

Delivery Games

1. Students should present unfamiliar material that has been parked on a lectern. They may not touch it. He who touches the lectern (or paper), sits down.
2. Two students present unfamiliar material simultaneously, battling for the attention of the audience. Rules: no shouting, no violence, no falling down.
3. Confiscate each student's prepared comments part way through. Judge them by how well they can finish from memory.

REVIEW QUESTIONS

1. Where should your feet be in the course of a talk?
2. What is the importance of posture?
3. Why is lighting important?
4. What should gestures not do?
5. What is the danger of affectation?

LESSON 30

Eye Contact

Remember that what you do with your eyes is a gesture and should be reckoned as such. But it is a very important gesture, one which we should consider separately. And so here we are, doing just that.

As the Beatles taught us, all you need is love. When a person is first learning to speak, it is easy (because of all the awkwardness) to become self-centered in the speaking. Put another way, how easy is it to be thinking, "Oh, dear—what shall they think!"? This being the case, it is also easy to slip off into a cocoon, from which the speaker attempts to articulate a series of muffled noises. A novice who is speaking, but who is doing so self-centeredly, will have difficulty making the kind of impression he needs to make.

And so, what do I mean, all you need is love? A speaker has the role of a matchmaker, a matchmaker who has genuine love and affection for the parties he is trying to fix up. A speaker's love and affection should be toward the material and toward the audience. The speaker wants the material and the audience to hit it off, and he wants the audience to go talk to the material's father.

Now a biblical principle here is that love bestows loveliness. If the speaker loves his material (or his treatment of that material), then the audience will love it for his sake—provided they love him, which they will if he loves them. But he is introducing the material to the audience, not the other way around. He is making the material winsome to the audience, not (usually) the other way around. This means something for the speaker's focus.

This is why it is not bad to look down at a set of notes—but how this is done makes all the difference. This is no more problematic than for a preacher to look to his text; he is *supposed* to look to his text. If he looks at the text because he has deficiencies, because he didn't care enough about the material to be familiar with it, then why should the audience want to become familiar with it? But if he looks to the text as a lover, with warm affection, then love bestows loveliness. How many times have we wanted to learn a subject, or pursue something for study, simply because someone we had high regard for had learned and appreciated it? And so this is what good teaching is: loving something in the presence of others.

We have both had instructors who picked a spot on the ceiling, stared at it, and recited material he had apparently learned twenty years before. Such professors know their material (and may have known it for many years), but it does not appear that they loved it at all. Nor does it appear that they care about their students. The students are nothing more than so many moo cows who have been somehow herded onto the great cattle cars of knowledge.

This does not mean a speaker must make eye contact with his material during the talk—if he has it memorized—but he does have to make clear through how he presents it that eye contact with his material is a very real (if previous) thing. The information is not being hauled out of a dusty storage bin, with the speaker showing surprise as it comes out. To change the metaphor, he is bringing it from the kitchen where he was the cook, and it is all still hot.

Eye contact does not mean eye contact with every last person in the room, nor does it mean eye contact with a select few in the audience. They have a corporate reality, and the speaker is looking at *them*. If he is not looking at the ceiling, or at their feet, or at just one spot two-thirds of the way back, then God has created us in such a way that eye contact takes care of itself. This is to say that the speaker does not have to establish eye contact. It is to say that he must not establish floor contact, or ceiling contact, or one-spot-on-the-back-wall contact. Let natural forces do the rest. Move the eyes where the people are.

Looking to the material can give a handy way of breaking eye contact in one place and moving to another. Whether a speaker is speaking to a large audience or a small one, he should look where the bulk of them

The head, being the chief member of the body, has a corresponding importance in delivery, serving not merely to produce graceful effect, but to illustrate our meaning as well.

—**Quintilian**, *Institutio Oratorio, vol. 4*

are. As a general rule, we would not recommend looking more than 45 degrees to the right or left.

But we should get back to the question of love. Love is treating others lawfully, from the heart. This means that if a man does as he would be done by, he has fulfilled the law and the prophets. What do we want when someone gets up to speak? The question does not concern topics necessarily, or particular gesticulations, but rather what we want in demeanor. If that is what we want, then that is what we should do.

SUGGESTED READING

1. Aristotle, *Rhetoric*, III.XVII.I—XIX.6
2. *Rhetorica Ad Herennium*, III.XI.19—III.XXIV.40
3. Quintilian, *Institutio Oratoria*, vol. 4, XII.III.I—X.19

EXERCISE

1. Write a 200 word descriptive sketch. Make it as smooth and interesting as possible. Now memorize it. Deliver it publicly without notes. Focus on keeping the constant eye contact fluid and natural. Don't glaze over while rooting through your mind for hints of the next sentence.

REVIEW QUESTIONS

1. What two things should a speaker love?
2. Is it bad to look down at a set of notes?
3. What is the best way to establish eye contact with the group as a whole?
4. What can looking at the material provide?
5. What should the range of motion be for making eye contact?

Putting It All Together

We do not travel from one aspect of this discipline to another, leaving the earlier aspect behind us. Rather, this whole enterprise is cumulative. And this means gathering up and keeping as much of what we have discussed as possible. And when peas start falling off the plate, make sure you go back and pick them up.

Speaking to others requires a real trust in the Lord. One of the most important things to do is to put the audience at ease by being at ease yourself. Comfort is contagious; confidence is contagious. And confidence comes from the Latin *con* and *fides,* which means "with faith." Faith in what? Faith in whom?

Faith in yourself is the root of either demagogy or spectacular failure. If a man is a demagogue, he can snooker some of the people some of the time, but right-minded observers will be put off by his cockiness. If he has faith in himself, or in his own native abilities, and that faith was perhaps misplaced, then the whole world will watch him do his face plant. Faith in God enables a speaker to be at ease for the sake of others. Confidence in this sense is an act of love.

A great temptation in this faces those who have good native abilities, and this is the temptation to coast. But as Moses told Israel somewhere in Numbers, and which all mothers should constantly quote to their children, be sure your sin will find you out. Do not coast. Even if you are not terrified, prepare as though you were. If you do not have time to prepare, and if you have to speak *ex tempore* anyway, and you are a roaring success in the presentation, learn to treat the event as a failure in your speaking career. Do not take perverse pride in being able to wing it. Kick yourself all the way home.

What use is a golden key, if it cannot unlock what we want to be unlocked, and what is wrong with a wooden one, if it can, since our sole aim is to open closed doors?
—**Saint Augustine,** *On Christian Teaching*

For oratory is like a river: the current is stronger when it flows within deep banks and with a mighty flood, than when the waters are shallow and broken by the pebbles that bar the way.
—**Quintilian,** *Institutio Oratorio, vol. 4*

This means practice, practice, practice. If it is likely (or possible) that you will be spending any significant amount of time speaking before others, then you want to take every opportunity to practice in order to hone your skills. As you do this, you are trying to put it all together, but do not try to put it all together all at once. Work at one thing until you get it down, or at least down enough to continue doing it, and then add another aspect of good rhetoric. And as a side note, unless you intend to homestead alone in the Montana wilderness, you will be spending a significant amount of time speaking in front of others every day of your life—ex temp, with no preparation, and without a lectern to protect you.

To repeat the same things again, Paul once said, was no trouble for him. Remember, you want three things to line up. You want convergence of ethos, pathos, and logos.

Logos—For diligent speakers, and especially for those diligent students who are not all that confident, the inclination is to put all your eggs in the basket of this content preparation. This is good; this you should have done without neglecting the other just-as-weighty matters of the law.

For my own part I would not hesitate to assert that a mediocre speech supported by all the power of delivery will be more impressive than the best speech unaccompanied by such power.
—**Quintilian,** *Institutio Oratorio, vol. 4*

Ethos—Give yourself to the cultivation of your character, which is to say, your sanctification. Do not wash the outside of the cup first, but you should get around to washing it. This goes back to our discussion of cultivated persona and the dangers of affectation. The problems attendant to this will be avoided if your first concern is that of worship, study, helping, giving, and so forth. If someone goes off to a good liberal arts college and comes back home with a tweed jacket with patches on the elbows, a pipe, and faux accent, and is twice as much of a snot as when he left home, the problem is ethos. Remember, a person cannot be a good speaker without being a good person, and this means that in the Christian worldview, ethos is holiness.

Pathos—We do not play with words, we work with them. And because we live in a fallen world, we fight dragons with them. Believe what you say, and say what you believe. And if you do not feel it at any level, this means you do not really believe it. This means there should be a correspondence between the content of what you are saying and how you are affected by it. Do not try to affect a group of hearers by anything that does not affect you first. If you shed false tears, then you are a manipulative, deceitful, treacherous hazard to the republic. Even if you do believe it, take care not to lurch into a manifestation of emotion. It may surprise you, and the audience, but when it does, it must be consistent with what went before. If it does not, then it will look like you were thinking, "I'm losing them. Better flip the choked-up switch."

There is no problem with practicing the mechanics of rhetoric. There is no hypocrisy whatever in practicing physical skills like voice projection, stance, gesture, eye contact, enunciation, and so forth. We have associated such things with artificiality because we have bought into the notion of spontaneity popularized by certain philosophical scoundrels. Then, because we practice such things a little, it does come off as stiff and artificial—and the charge of affectation sticks. Which it ought not.

And as you go out in the great wide world, to speak to audiences with their mouths agape—where did this personage get this wisdom?—remember that if they trace any of it back to your reading of this book, we will deny everything.

> All emotional appeals will inevitably fall flat, unless they are given the fire that voice, look, and the whole carriage of the body can give them.
> —**Quintilian**, *Institutio Oratorio, vol. 4*

> Thus the works of the orator will be great not extravagant, sublime not bombastic, bold not rash, severe but not gloomy, grace but not slow, rich but not luxuriant, pleasing but not effeminate, grand but not grandiose.
> —**Quintilian**, *Institutio Oratorio, vol. 4*

SUGGESTED READING

I. Quintilian, *Institutio Oratoria*, vol. 4, XII.X.20—XI.31

EXERCISE

I. Compose a 1500–2000 word speech, following the classical structure. Target a hostile audience but keep your tone light and your style interesting. Remember . . . everything. Present publicly. Sit down when the applause dies.

REVIEW QUESTIONS

1. In what sense is the universe a figure of speech? And in what sense is it not?
2. How is the Logos important to this question?
3. How does the created order speak about God?
4. Why are all things "cognates"?
5. What makes effective metaphor possible?
6. Why is the poet a "seer" more than a maker?
7. Can anything therefore be a metaphor for anything else?
8. How should the discipline of seeing metaphor begin?
9. How is the hypostatic union important to metaphor?
10. How does one's hermeneutic relate to the question of learning to speak with metaphorical richness?
11. Give an example of a motif. How about a scriptural motif?
12. What does it mean to learn metaphor by imitation?
13. How can you profit through imitation?
14. What is elocution?
15. What are the elements of elocution?
16. Be prepared to define each.
17. What is the relationship of musical instruments and public speaking?
18. How should you begin to discipline your gestures?
19. What is the danger of affectation?
20. What is the role of love in public speaking?
21. What are some of the mechanics of eye contact?
22. What is confidence?
23. Be prepared to discuss the relations (again) of logos, ethos, and pathos.
24. What is the danger for speakers who are naturally gifted?
25. What is the danger for speakers who are not?

In the art of rhetoric, then, there is no more. All these faculties we shall attain if we supplement the precepts of theory with diligent practice.
—*Rhetorica Ad Herrennium*

APPENDIX

Language Study and Copiousness

One of the best ways to improve your copiousness in English is through the study of other languages, particularly Latin. As was argued in *Recovering the Lost Tools of Learning*,[1] there are five basic reasons for studying Latin, and all of them are related to copiousness in some way. The first is that the study of Latin refines a student's grasp of *English.* The second is that the study of Latin is a great aid as a student grows to appreciate literature. Ancient literature is included in this, but the many classical allusions found in *English* literature are also in view. Third, the study of Latin helps the student understand the infancy of our civilization. The fourth reason is that it trains the student in precision of mind, which will enable that student to excel in scientific studies. The last reason given is that the study of Latin is an excellent platform from which to begin studying other modern languages, particularly the Romance languages which are descended from Latin. With these reasons (particularly with the fourth), it is assumed that in their studies the students will progress as far as systematic translation of many of the ancient texts. But fluidity in translation is the means to these other ends, not the end itself.

So, that said, what *is* the general trajectory of learning Latin, and what should you be aiming for? Here is a broad-brush overview of the basic stages:

I. *Grammatical knowledge* can be described as an abstract knowledge of the rules of Latin grammar, along with enough of a working vocabulary to provide grist for the grammatical mill. For example, the student knows enough nouns to have something to attach his noun endings

---

I. Douglas Wilson, *Recovering the Lost Tools of Learning: An Approach to Distinctively Christian Education* (Wheaton: Crossway Books, 1991).

to, as well as to be able to fashion simple, illustrative sentences. *Femina poetam amat.*

2. *Deciphering ability* would include a functioning knowledge of Latin grammar and, given a dictionary, an ability to "decode" a new passage. The student would perhaps have a reserve of 500 to 1000 words that he would not have to look up.

3. *Fluidity* in Latin would include a functioning knowledge of Latin grammar and an immediate grasp of Latin meanings without having to "decode" new material. The student functions smoothly and well, like a native speaker, but only within the artificial world created for him to work in. Within this narrow world, students are able to read, converse in, compose, and think in Latin.

4. *Native fluency* would include an instinctive knowledge of Latin grammar, as well as an immediate grasp of at least 10,000 words. Someone with this ability could be dropped for a couple of weeks into ancient Rome and get along fine, at least with regard to all the functions of ordinary life. No student in an average Latin program will achieve this kind of fluency through their studies unless they have taken extraordinary measures on their own time to supplement what is taught. All four levels are an extraordinary help in achieving copiousness in English.

Of course, it is fair to state that it is assumed here that any student who decides to go on to study Latin at a collegiate or professional level (in order to acquire fluency in Latin) should have been well-equipped by this kind of education to do so. But a basic course in a language like Latin does not give fluency in Latin. It does improve copiousness in English. Given the hours available for language instruction in a standard school, true fluency in the Latin language is *not* within reach. Fluency in English can be determined (roughly) by the average number of vocabulary words that the average speaker of English knows, which is somewhere between 12,000 and 20,000 words. Let's take the low number of 12,000 and compare that to the number of vocabulary words that a Latin student would usually have if he remembered every word that he was ever taught throughout the course of his instruction. That would give him a working vocabulary of around three thousand words. Since it is likely that he will not remember them all, the number will be somewhat lower, let us say 2,500 words. This is about one fifth of the vocabulary of an ancient Roman car mechanic, and we have to recall that *he* was on the low end of that society. So true Latin fluency is not the goal and cannot realistically be the goal of any standard school curriculum. True fluency in a language cannot really be achieved apart from complete immersion in that language world.

The central goal, therefore, is to provide the students with the *tools* of language learning, enabling them to learn for themselves as they have opportunity and desire. They may want to write novels (or yea, even screenplays) in English, and their education should equip them how to master that skill—one that was never taught to them explicitly. They may want to design and build bridges, and their basic education should have taught them how to think, so that they can excel when they come to subjects they were never actually taught explicitly. And they may want to go on to become masters of the Latin language—and what they were taught in high school should serve as a set of tools that will help them do that. But if, five years after graduation, the alumni are very rusty with their translation abilities if handed a copy of *Gallic Wars*, this does not mean that their years of Latin were a waste. That was not the goal.

The situation is comparable to learning how to play various musical instruments. A school should provide basic music instruction and equip the student with the tools he needs to pursue it further. His musical instruction should identify giftedness in that area and should give the parents and student what they need in order to take advantage of that giftedness. But "fluency" in music would require extreme dedication on the part of the student *outside* of school in order to get the levels of immersion required.

Not all subjects are created equal. Mastery of math is a very different thing than mastery of history, and mastery of history is a very different thing than mastery of English composition. Mastery of English composition is very different than mastery of prose literature and poetry. All high school courses have two basic goals. The first is what we might call a *platform goal*, and the second is what we might call the *continuing competence goal*. Rhetoric and communication is a platform goal. No matter where a student is eventually called in life, they will also be called to communicate effectively and, as servants of the Word, have love for and abilities with words.

A platform goal works this way. When parents enroll their child in kindergarten, they do not know that child's life vocation and calling. When they see to it that the child is provided with a good, general education, K-12, they are establishing a process that will identify that child's strengths and weaknesses and which will build on the former and correct and strengthen the latter. This will mean that the child and his parents will be in a much better position to decide what vocational direction to pursue, and they will be able to do this without any handicaps thrown in the way by an inadequate high school education. The graduates are equipped to move on to college, knowing what platform they have decided to build on, and they are able to take it from there. All of them were equipped by their primary and secondary education, and none of them were hindered by it. In this sense, a Latin program also contributes to this platform—which means that students are equipped to pursue, if they so desire, a college degree in classics. This does not mean that every student should want to do so, or even be able to—any more than any student should be able to go on to get a PhD in math.

The continuing competence goal is that of providing the students with a basic toolbox that they will personally need throughout the rest of their lives—when they are balancing their checkbook, helping their fifth grader with his science homework, reading the Bible to the family, talking to the kids around the dinner table about the significance of the Fourth of July, or reading magazines with articles that have phrases like *mutatis mutandis* in them. This is a very general education, designed to be used and never forgotten in the course of an ordinary life. With this goal, for example, a good Latin program enables an average graduate to understand a much broader range of English vocabulary, the structure of basic grammar, and the occasional Latin phrase. It develops copiousness.

The study of Latin is immensely valuable, but it is not an end, *but rather a means to more copious students and effective communicators.* The end goal for a Latin program is *not* fluency in Latin for every student. Rather, this means that the curriculum that pursues *fluidity* in Latin conversation and translation (for all students who pass the course) is a means to another end. A student could put down his Latin text at the end of tenth grade and resolve never to think about it consciously again, and this would not mean that we had failed with him. He has still been shaped by the process of education he has been through, broadened in his instincts, and it will not be possible for him to walk away from *that*. He will always know (for the rest of his life) that *diction* has to do with speaking, that *valedictory* addresses are speaking a farewell, that *benedictions* are a blessing and that *maledictions* are not.

English is covered with Velcro—it is the kind of language that picks up other words and phrases readily. A student who wants to increase in copiousness should pick his books carefully, and his courses at the university carefully. If he is in the right place at the right time, a lot of this process will take care of itself.